Theater at the Margins

THEATER: Theory/Text/Performance

Enoch Brater, Series Editor
University of Michigan

Theater at the Margins

Text and the
Post-Structured Stage

Erik MacDonald

Ann Arbor

THE UNIVERSITY OF MICHIGAN PRESS

Copyright © by the University of Michigan 1993
All rights reserved
Published in the United States of America by
The University of Michigan Press
Manufactured in the United States of America

1996   1995   1994   1993   4   3   2   1

Library of Congress Cataloging-in-Publication Data

MacDonald, Erik.
    Theater at the margins : text and the post-structured stage / Erik
MacDonald.
       p.   cm. — (Theater—theory, text, performance)
    Includes bibliographical references and index.
    ISBN 0-472-10311-3
    1. Experimental theater. 2. Experimental drama—History and
criticism. 3. Postmodernism (Literature) 4. Deconstruction.
5. Theater—Philosophy. 6. Theater and society.   I. Title.
PN2193.E86M33   1993
792'.022—dc20   93-29786
                                                            CIP

A CIP catalogue record for this book is available from the British Library.

For Carolyn

Acknowledgments

I owe a lot to many people for this book. My first and last thanks are to Carolyn Talarr for her generous suggestions and revisions of this work as well as much needed psychological and moral support. She will always have my deepest gratitude. I am grateful for the comments of my friends and colleagues in Seattle, San Francisco, Los Angeles, and Milwaukee, including Michael Olenick, Bill Mayer, Oran Walker, Terry Amidei, David Bishop, Steven Shaviro, Esther Beth Sullivan, Matt Silverstein, Barry Witham, Jon Lutterbie, Kate Cummings, Paoli Lacy, dede moyse, Jeff Raz, Maria Timoroas, Larry Williams, Al Grossman, Andy Bush, Linda Hammett, Kathleen Woodward, Vicki Patraka, Rover, and Aja. Some portions of this book have appeared in the *Journal of Dramatic Theory and Criticism* and *Essays in Theatre*. I would also like to thank the National Endowment for the Humanities for a fellowship during the summer of 1991 that allowed me the time to rethink this project. At the University of Michigan Press, Christina L. Milton's and LeAnn Fields's support were invaluable. I'd like to thank Sue-Ellen Case for guiding me through many first drafts at the University of Washington; Herbert Blau was especially generous in reading a version during the summer of 1991; Timothy Murray not only provided the initial impetus for writing something like this book way back when but also has been unfailingly encouraging throughout. His tireless comments made revision easy. Finally, this book is for Carolyn, who is in every page.

Contents

CHAPTER 1

On the Margins:
Post-Structuralist Theater

There is no official decree or supernatural intervention which graciously dispenses the theatre from the demands of theoretical reflection.
—Roland Barthes, *Critical Essays*

Whatever way you turn you have not even *started* thinking.
—Antonin Artaud, *Oeuvres complètes*

Since we have already said everything, the reader must bear with us if we continue on awhile. If we extend ourselves by force of play. If we then *write* a bit.
—Jacques Derrida, *Plato's Pharmacy*

In the dominant theater tradition, the written text is the primary vehicle for making sense. While scenographic and aural "texts" also structure the theatrical event, the "dramatic" text is central. Yet how does the dramatic text make sense? How does it contrive the "truth" of a theatrical event? More important, especially if one reads Artaud seriously, what does "making sense" mean? What dramaturgical events constitute the scene of "sense making"? "Making sense" assumes not only an audience (for whom does the text/performance/ event make sense? what sort of sense? who is served by the sense that is made?—crucial questions in a society in which knowledge is power), but also a text/vehicle endowed with certain properties legitimated in some way to convey meaning. (Indeed, these are concerns pertinent to any text in the theater, dramatic, scenographic, acoustic, or otherwise.) The questions that Derrida asks, "what is a text? and what must the psyche be if it can be represented by a text?" (1978, 199), intimate that "a text" is the primary structure of the psyche and, as a result, serves as the representational account of experience. Based on the assertion that a "constructed" text, rather than an originary essence, is the fundamental apparatus by which the psyche operates, post-structuralist thought considers textuality as an apparatus that directly participates in the production of meaning and in the formation of structure, rather than a monolith that guides and structures "meaning" while remaining separate from it. Consequently, post-structuralist thought (which includes more than "Derrida") suggests that "texts" interpret events and make sense of experience. By asking what sort of structures comprise the text and, further, what hidden ruses or mechanisms, whether ideological, historical, or political in nature, compel it faithfully (or faithlessly) to re-produce a teleological, if not religious, experience—as if truth is there to be grabbed in the unveiling of the text—post-structuralism attempts to open the text to the widest possible array of interpretations.[1]

One of the major areas of post-structuralist inquiry—deconstruction—explores the text as a site where meanings are put into play with one another rather than systematized into a hierarchy. Deconstruction's project of delaying the closure of representation by problematizing the appearance of meaning finds reflection in the theater as well. In fact, the imposition of "meaning" (in the sense of one fixed "right answer") that deconstruction resists so vigorously is also antithetical to the theater and theatricality. "To Hide, to Show: that is theatricality. But the modernity of our fin-de-siècle is due to this: there is nothing to be replaced, no lieutenancy is legitimate, or else all are; the replacing—therefore the meaning—is itself only a substitute for displacement" (Lyotard 1976, 105). In Lyotard's view, meaning in theater is an external imposition. The quest for meaning, then, is something of a pathological response to the inability to ever be sure about appearances. Indeed, it is not possible to trust the simple appearance of meaning in a realm defined by "hiding and showing," for it is never certain exactly what to trust as "correct."

In this context, Luigi Pirandello's plays are outstanding examples of this struggle (though by no means are they historically the first to recognize this concern). For instance, by questioning the factuality of any stable identity, Henry in *Henry IV* successfully challenges the assumption that the individual must assume a given social role and that to do otherwise is a sure sign of insanity. In all Pirandello's plays, the certainty of social identity is revealed as a contingent, rather than an a priori, determinant. Yet the illusions that Pirandello's characters encounter and dispel in attempting to discern the truth of any given appearance rest in a fundamentally stable linguistic world and are conveyed by a text that depends on a well-ordered relationship between things and words (i.e., that words have exact meanings). Pirandello's plays, for example, disrupt the outer world of appearances by questioning the truth of self-revelatory statements; in doing so, they display a primary feature of theatricality and theater in a manner similar to how deconstruction perturbates the binary linguistic assumptions on which the text is based (i.e., deconstruction recognizes that words themselves cannot be trusted to mean any one thing). In one sense, theater texts have always embodied an awareness of their own margins that contributes directly to their theatricality, for, if "theatricality" is inherent to the dramatic text, then somewhere in the text is also an antistructural force that opens the text to Derridian concerns. With this in mind, what sort of readings would be possible if the theatrical (outward) and deconstructive (inward) impulses were matched? What might arise if the textual assumptions of a mode of writing that radically questions its world were themselves interrogated from the perspective of the slippage within that world's own defining terms?

This approach asks how "production" (whether onstage or in reading/writing) creates or reveals (particular) meanings, of what competing interpretations are possible, and how, indeed, more than one understanding of the text can be present at any given moment. Texts are not univocal; approaching the theater with the assumption that there is a "correct" way to read any particular text is a mistake. Derrida's invocation to "continue on awhile" should prove medicinal to any search for the ultimate meaning of a text: "a text is not a text unless it hides from its first comer, from the first glance, the law of its composition and the rules of its game. A text remains, moreover, forever imperceptible" (Derrida 1982a, 63). It should be remembered that writing, imagined by Plato to be a remedy, or *pharmakon,* cuts two ways: as cure and as poison, as Derrida relentlessly shows in *Dissemination* and elsewhere. As the representative of a speaking presence (i.e., the father), the text can represent either faithfully or unfaithfully the off-stage presence: the "father" both needs writing to convey his voice when he is not there and should for that very reason fear writing for its ability to be misinterpreted. Caught between these possibilities, of supplementing and supplanting the living presence, writing maintains an essential theatricality, a *différance* that continually conceals its identity.[2] This is precisely the struggle that Pirandello's characters face, but with the distinction that deconstruction focuses on the foundational or teleological structures that impel a text's sense-making apparatus.

Posing the question about the particular role and mechanics of the dramatic text onstage raises larger questions as well—questions of how narratives are constructed, of the structural organization of a particular text, and of what "meanings" are produced by certain structures.

> The stage is theological for as long as its structure, following the entirety of tradition, comports the following elements: an author-creator who, absent and from afar, is armed with a text and keeps watch over, assembles, regulates the time or the meaning of representation, letting the latter represent him as concerns what is called the content of his thoughts, his intentions, his ideas. (Derrida 1978, 235)

Derrida's apparent dismissal of Western theater's metaphysical project in "The Theatre of Cruelty and the Closure of Representation" still has not been fully accounted for within the theater, even in productions in which the playwright is replaced by the director. His point that a theater that does not question its limits—does not question the limits of representation—remains frozen within the economy of fathers and sons, of author-creators. This point also suggests that the "cult of the playwright" that obsesses contemporary theater signals a retrogression to an inherently more conservative stage. Even after a generation of attacks, deconstructions, and dismemberments of the Author-playwright and the text and despite their countless desecrations in the theater and performance art of the 1960s, 1970s, and 1980s, their return seems inexplicable except in the light of this fatal strategy of representation. While Derrida goes on to ends far different from simply condemning theater, that the theater might be based on Platonic notions of textuality suggests that it might also have a close relationship to the political and social institutions, which share similar foundations, that have arisen in the West.

As part of this study, I am taking for granted that the dramatic text is a central element of theater, and, while there are certainly other elements that deserve at least as much attention and that also contain their own historicities, I am primarily interested in the text's architectonics. If, as Lacan would say, the unconscious is structured like a language, then it should be understandable why, despite an intense amount of theater and performance that tried to do away with, avoid, or ignore the text, the text did indeed return in the 1980s with such a vengeance. Maybe the text never really left the theater. Certainly the traditional dramatic text, written by an Author whose certainty and presence are assured, was rejected during the 1960s and 1970s; but the fact that it did return, however bracketed, and certainly not just in the conventional theater, suggests that "the dramatic text" accords a structure that is crucial to the theatrical event and that, furthermore, cannot be simply willed away once and for all. Even in the work of Robert Wilson, whose performances are often cited as "deconstructive," the text retains a certain "textuality" that does not disappear by removing its more traditional features. In fact, what passes for "deconstruction" in this sense often ends up as a simplistic suspension of the philosophical concerns of deconstruction and post-structuralism for a referentless joyride through a value-free theater that reenforces the very ideological conceits that the work presumes to examine.[3] This criticism is not intended to argue for only a text-based theater or to suggest that the dramatic text is the most important element in the theater or even that it is the only one worthy of an academic study such as this one. Again, following Lacan's disavowal of a "true" human nature (the unconscious is structured *like* a language), my concentration on the text herein signals a certain incompleteness, a deferral of belief or conviction that I, as a critic, can surmise all the threads of the theatrical event and pass a final judgment of any sort.[4]

The last thirty years of textual and cultural criticism, as well as performance art and "avant-garde" theater experiments—much of which has challenged the text's hegemony as sovereign signifier—suggest that the text is a central juncture for theoretical reflection on the theater. By initiating a critique of representation, post-structuralism goes well beyond either passive acceptance or outright abandonment, for it recognizes a certain difference and displacement in representation, a slippage in the place of an inexorable "heart," or presence, of what is represented.

> Because it has always already begun, representation therefore has no end. But one can conceive of the closure of that which is without end. . . . To think the closure of representation is to think the tragic: not as the representation of fate, but as the fate of representation. . . . And it is to think why it is *fatal* that, in its closure, representation continues. (Derrida 1978, 250)

At the limits of representation is a caesura that prevents the text from ever fully representing itself, from ever standing outside its own structure or investments, for that moment would signify originary presence, a condition whose impossibility closure must mask. Accordingly, meaning depends on the establishment of an arbitrary means to end representation, on a connection between signifier and signified that not only allows but demands closure. Where there is meaning, there will also be closure. In this model (which is not so monolithic as to allow only one "truth"), there is very little room for play or indeterminacy, except perhaps "at the margins" of the text.[5]

Putting "play" at the margins of a text is not as simple a process as it might seem, for it raises the question of what constitutes a margin, of how the margin can be set, and, further, of what relationship a "margin" might have to the "center." Certainly, there are margins, or edges, around the limit of the stage, sometimes bounded by black panels or cloth, off of which actors sometimes fall if they venture out too far. Beyond this physical boundary, the margins of theater are themselves a matter of some debate. How to set them? Is "margin" to be equated with *marginalism*, a ploy whereby, according to Daryl Chin, any meaning or intention can find a place, as it were, through an "accreditation of these additional perspectives by defining a dominant, and ceding territory to the sidelines" (164)? If this is the case, any production, regardless of content or form, could assert its marginality simply by claiming a difference from an imagined "center." But, again, it is not simply a matter of replacing one center with another or maintaining a world that imbues margins and centers with one-to-one (or two-, or three-, etc., to-one) relationships. I linger on this point because the margins constitute a playing field, a theatrical (and theoretical) space whose fundamental composition is indeed at issue, rather than composing a unified universe in which the drama is played out. This is especially true if the theater is to be removed from questions of ontology, theology, or (Platonic) hierarchy. Indeed, perhaps Plato banished theater from his ideal Republic because the theater, in the final analysis, continually refuses to tell its own truth, which, logically, precludes it from deciding on its own margin.

In fact, the margins on which theater—and textuality —takes place represent something other than simply an edge, boundary, or position within a hierarchy that reproduces a static relationship to a "center stage." The margin, in the sense I am using it here, is a limit at which the text encounters, among other things, its philosophical "Other." In this space, doubled understandings (at the intersection of Same/Other) appear as folds in the text, revealing in the process that there is always some degree of play within the text. These folds, which illuminate for a moment the fundamental elements that constitute a text, provide not a way to the "soul" of a work but, rather, to a theatrical margin that constructs textuality as the play within and between "hiding and showing."

> Overflows and cracks: that is, on the one hand compels us to count in its margin more and less than one believes is said or read, an unfolding due to the structure of the mark (which is the same word as *marche*, as limit, and as *margin*); and on the other hand, luxates the very body of statements in the pretensions to univocal rigidity or regulated polysemia. A lock opened to a double understanding no longer forming a single system. Which does not

amount to acknowledging that the margin maintains itself within and without. (Derrida 1982b, xxiv)

There is always some degree of play on the margins of a text. According to Derrida, illuminating the "very body of statements" that composes the philosophical certainty of a text reveals a constant struggle with the Other, with the "statements" that are perforce excluded or rejected in the quest for "univocal rigidity." Consequently, any "text," whether written for the theater or not, is at this level a "dramatic text," for the margin of a text implies an intransigent form of action. Obviously, not all texts are dramatic in any traditional sense, but what Derrida intimates is that, within the folds of a text, there is always more or less of a degree of doubleness that facilitates multiple possible meanings. Furthermore, by asserting that "a text is not a text unless it hides . . . the law of its composition and the rules of its game" (Derrida), it is easy to see how the text's theatricality implies a fundamental chaos in place of any "heart" or textual foundation.

The "folds" that constitute margins in the passage quoted above signal a certain displacement, or deferral, of exact one-to-one correspondences between meanings and structures. At the same time, these deferrals and displacements begin to look suspiciously like a stage performance, as if there may be a doubleness in words and things that renders questions about the "essential nature" of a text meaningless. How then to explore forms of writing that present an awareness of this inherent theatricality of the margin?

To write otherwise. To delimit the space of a closure no longer analogous to what philosophy can represent for itself under this name, according to a straight or circular line enclosing a homogeneous space. To determine, entirely against any philosopheme, the intransigence that prevents it from calculating its margin. (xxiv–xxv)

For a text to activate, almost self-reflectively, the margin, is for it to militate against the determinations of sense-making apparatus. The spaces inhabited by the dramatic texts that I will attempt to situate on the margins of theater are ones that question, upset, or discard their ontopolitical inheritance in such a way that it (the text) can calculate that intransigence that enslaves the text according to some philosophical jurisdiction. "In the beginning there was the word. Now there is only suspicion" (Blau 1982, 45). For the most part, the theater texts that I read in the following chapters maintain an openness at their margins and an awareness of the word's "onstage" transience.

The "margin," therefore, is similar to what Artaud had in mind in calling for a theater that retains a sense of the significance of the struggle for meaning: "We are not free. And the sky can still fall on our heads. And the theatre has been created to teach us that first of all" (1958, 79). By presenting transhistorical notions of "value," or "truth," according to already accepted aesthetic forms, the theater is relieved from historically or politically specific concerns. Yet there are consequences of the margin that must be taken into account, for, when philosophy reaches its margins, it is confronted with its double. This double—which is the shadow of all the possibilities not explored—is what gives theater its sociohistorical connection, is what traces, in every movement onstage, the history of that possible movement. It is not a history that is the simple onstage recollection of facts but, rather, as Philippe Lacoue-Labarthe argues, "the possibility of History," which contains the cultural, political, and social structures of a particular "people" within its very language formations (a point I explore in chapter 4). It was in this sense of the "historial" that Artaud wanted to put an end to the antiseptic timelessness of beautiful art by reminding the theater that, no matter which way it turns, it still must think its own "historiality."

If in fact we raise the question of the origins and *raison d'être* (or primordial necessity) of the theatre, we find, metaphysically, the materialization or rather the exteriorization of a kind of essential drama which would contain, in a manner at once manifold and unique, the essential principles of all drama, already *disposed* and *divided*, not so much as to lose their character as principles, but

enough to comprise, in a substantial and active fashion (i.e., res-
onantly), an infinite perspective of conflicts. (1958, 50)

This "infinite perspective of conflicts" on the margin, before the text
settles into a univocal rigidity, will haunt the theater until it takes
into account that, at any juncture, there is a multiplicity of possible
choices. In the confusion of seen and unseen apparatus, among the
shadows and ghosts of "the possibility of History," the text is performed, even while this configuration of play is a long way from
simply the words on a page or in an actor's mouth. In the Artaudian
world, which is the world of philosophy's Other, play is imbricated
in language to such a degree that language itself, whether spoken or
written, is indispensable.

That the dramatic text might be a central element in the theater
does not imply that it lacks other institutional structures and investments. One result of contemporary theories of textuality is the ero-
sion of the belief that a text conveys an essential "truth." It is hard
to imagine today the separation of "truth" and language or to imagine
that either is free of political determinants. Yet these are points that
still need to be stressed, that should not be forgotten if the text or the
theater is to escape its ongoing ontotheological heritage and, furthermore, remember its historial responsibilities.

The concern with historiality—with, as Michael Hays puts it, "how
the theatre and theatrical process can be viewed as systems of signification which form a 'rhetoric' that describes the social configuration
in which the theatre of a given epoch develops" (1977, 85)—is not
limited to theory. Bertolt Brecht made central the relationship between structure and history in his productions and texts. Brecht's
interests in theater are well documented elsewhere and are in a sense
tangential to my argument here. It is worthwhile, however, to note
that his interest in uncovering the hidden dynamics of the theater is
preeminently a search for the political effects of meaning onstage.
Hays's understanding of the processes of history in the production
of meaning is particularly apt to a discussion of Brecht: "It is . . . the
dialectical tension existing between the parts of the theatrical event
and between present and past theatrical practice as a whole that

must be examined if we wish to perceive the historically grounded process of change in the theater" (97). Throughout his career, Brecht attempted to create structures that would account for the role of history in political process. The *verfremdungseffekt* (alienation effect), for example, foregrounds the separation between representation and actuality and thus is part of Brecht's project to force the audience into a confrontation with the underlying political affiliations of the theatrical apparatus. Brecht's texts are grounded on the assumption that maintaining a critical relationship between the various elements onstage, including the relationship between stage and audience, creates a wider, more complete understanding of the political implications of the various social structures also represented onstage. In foregrounding the manner by which structure produces meaning, his texts call attention to the political dimensions of social relations and reveal political agendas in seemingly benign relationships. By focusing on the structure of relationships, most specifically on their class or economic aspects, his texts disrupt the categorical assumptions of the theatrical apparatus and question the implied relationships within any social order. Yet it is not simply a matter of "putting politics onstage" in a didactic or simplistic fashion. Perhaps the key to Brecht's importance is his ability to provide a "thick description" of the individual's implication in political systems. In his late plays such as *Mother Courage*, *The Good Person of Setzwan*, or *Galileo*, for instance, Brecht focuses (more or less) on the individual not to recreate the narrative of one person's life (à la realism) but, rather, to explore the mechanisms by which the individual is caught up in historial processes.

Roland Barthes notes that in Brecht's insistence on the constructed nature of theater is an incipient understanding of history-making mechanisms: "The whole of Brecht's dramaturgy is subject to a necessity of *distance*, and the essence of the theater is staked on the perpetuation of this distance: it is not the success of any particular dramatic style which is in question, it is the spectator's consciousness and hence his capacity to make history" (1972, 34–35). This sense of distance is critical to Brecht, for it makes apparent the idea that the individuals portrayed are part of larger historiopolitical structures that determine their actions to a much greater degree than any theology of "free will" (a will that, in the final analysis, is itself contingent upon the individual's place in a social structure). In understanding the historiality of texts and theater in this way, both Brecht and Barthes seek to "demythologize" social apparatus by emphasizing that meaning and truth are by-products of structure, rather than vice versa.

In a structuralist theater project with radically different political investments from that of Brecht, Michael Kirby attempts to free structure of meaning, or value, completely. Kirby differentiates between "referential" and "nonreferential" theater: "It is this theatre of thematic meaning, of 'aboutness' . . . that I will call 'referential theatre.' Theatre that does not have a message, contains no intellectual theme, is not 'about' life, I will call 'nonreferential theatre' " (1987, 34). Kirby, who was instrumental in documenting underground performance in the 1960s, introduced "Happenings" to larger theater audiences. By basing his practice and writings on the aesthetics of Happenings, that is, on the idea that anything can be considered performance if placed in the right context, Kirby calls attention to the importance of structure in the fundamental constitution of theatrical events and brings a sense of indeterminacy to the theater.[6] Kirby finds in "structuralist theater" a method for understanding the interrelated elements of performance on their own terms, in relation to one another, without external judgment. Toward this end, he theorizes a "nonreferential theater" that takes structuralist theater to its extreme by making the elements of performance have relevance only within a closed system. Rather than assuming that there needs to be any connection with the external world, Kirby wants to create a stage experience as a hermetically sealed event, one separated from the concerns that underscore Brecht's plays, for example:

The most difficult problems in [creating structuralist performance] relate to meaning. If a performance has no meaning—as in music and dance—it is relatively easy to make structure predominate. In drama, however, structure has long been used to support and clarify meaning. Therefore, where meaning exists, it tends to take over. The spectator assumes that, since there are semantic elements, the presentation should be understood semantically. Material is interpreted; meanings are "read in" where they were not intended. (112)[7]

Of his performance *Revolutionary Dance*, which consisted of several scenes of people engaged in civil war in several different countries, Kirby insists that, because the setting was "international," his cast multiracial, and the action nonspecific, this constituted a nonreferential performance and that any attempt to make it "meaningful" (as one critic did) is mistaken: "For the Structuralist trying to design particular experiences, the tendency for meaning to become ascendant is a problem that must be considered" (113). Unlike Brecht, who sought to associate structure with politics, Kirby remains convinced that politics in any form has to do with "meaning" and thus is inherently an external construction, placed on the theater performance from outside and should be ignored: "[A] political view of theatre is intellectual. It does not deal with theatre as a personal, sensory . . . experience. . . . Personal sensations have no social or political aspect." Kirby discards meaning and interpretation in the search for a "nonsemiotic" theater: "In theatrical terms, one content or message is not better or worse than another" (88). Whereas Brecht and Barthes saw structure as the foundation for a political critique, Kirby sees structure and structuralist theater as a way to avoid the question of history by imposing a timeless aestheticism on the work that frees it from any referentiality. In this way, Kirby's work exemplifies certain dangers in an uncritical fascination with structure to the exclusion of all other things.

At the same time Brecht was implementing his political notions of a structuralist theater, Gertrude Stein was also investigating structure onstage, but her focus was on the word's phenomenological status, its existence as an event in and of itself. By focusing on the sign as an artifact, rather than a transparent medium, Stein disrupted the assumption that experience outside, or unmediated by, language is possible. In *Listen to Me* Stein uses language to conflate words, objects, and ideas in order to call attention to the impossibility of constructing meaning outside of language. The characters never go beyond their linguistic construction, instead they produce "meaning" in the surface exchange of words:

> Sweet William is careful not to say that Acts are altogether he is
> very careful to say that he is not very sorry he is very careful to say
> that he is not very careful of their feelings he is very careful of their
> feelings he is very sorry he does say that Acts are not altogether
> That is what Sweet William is he is careful to say that Acts are not
> altogether. (Stein 1975, 418)

What Sweet William talks about is left unspecified; rather than recollecting an action or event, the narration becomes its own object through the repetition of linguistic patterns, phrases, and words. In *Listen to Me*, Stein accomplishes a breakdown of the distance between things and their representatives, words, a relationship that implies a hierarchy between the two.[8] In this way, the play bears some resemblance to the work of two structural linguists who were contemporaries of Stein: Charles S. Peirce and Ferdinand de Saussure.

Saussure paved the way for later theater semiotics by calling attention to the binomial characteristics of language. Every word is, according to Saussure, a sign that consists of a signifier (word) and signified (thing). Language consists of these signifiers that stand in for or represent their respective signifieds. Meaning is created through the interlocking patterns of signifiers that make up a language. Peirce complicated the model by identifying three categories of signifiers: the index, icon, and symbol. For Saussure and Peirce, as well as Stein, meaning obtains through the interrelationships of these sign systems, rather than in the relationship of words to actual extralinguistic material or phenomena. While the individual theories are more complex than I can present here, the basic idea that meaning and reference are linguistically based (and therefore, Michael Kirby notwithstanding, inescapable) created the field of semiotics, or the study of structure in language. This field is of vast importance to theater studies, as exemplified by Jiri Veltrusky's statement in 1940 that "all that is on stage is a sign" (1964, 84).

Stein's implicit interest in structural linguistics, or semiotics, coincides with a more contemporary interest in the construction of meaning onstage. While this is indeed one of semiotics' primary aims, it sounds surprisingly like a structuralist approach. It could be said that, while semiotics concentrates on linguistic structures, structuralism focuses on the various elements of the stage event. Yet this distinction is tenuous at best, for, if "everything on the stage is a sign," as every theater semiologist since Veltrusky would agree, structure has to be a semiological element. Jonathan Culler's comment that "it would not be wrong to suggest that structuralism and semiology are identical" (8) exemplifies the difficulty in differentiating the two. One thing that can be said is that "structuralist theater" actually refers to a specific historical theater (e.g., Kirby's), and semiotics, as a linguistic-based theoretical perspective, has been used more as a method for "reading theater." This distinction roughly follows Terry Eagleton's suggestion in *Literary Theory: An Introduction* that structuralism is a method and semiotics a field.

From the Prague school linguists in the 1930s and 1940s, who founded their semiotics on the basis of Saussure's work, and who were the first organized "school" to explore theater semiotics in a rigorous, almost formulaic fashion, several second- and third-generation semiologists have taken their understanding of the sign as a basic unit of signification and have furthermore suggested that the composite theater experience is a "cybernetic machine" (Barthes) that can be broken down into fundamental units for analysis: "The nature of the theatrical sign, whether analogical, symbolic or conventional, the denotation and connotation of the message—all these fundamental problems of semiology are in the theatre" (Barthes 1972, 262).

In *The Semiotics of Theater and Drama*, Kier Elam picks up on Barthes's concern with the sign in suggesting that semiotics is a science dedicated to studying the structure and production of communication systems: "It is—ideally, at least—a multidisciplinary science whose precise methodological characteristics will necessarily vary from field to field but which is united by a common global concern, the better understanding of our own meaning-bearing behavior" (1). He proceeds to break down the theater into a succession of codes that formulate dramatic action, time, and performance in a systematized fashion. By analyzing the theatrical event as a multitude of interrelated components, Elam attempts to understand how, in the interaction of the carefully delineated pieces, an overall effect is produced, even in the face of the apparent incompleteness of any "dramatological" analysis. What he discovers as a result is that theater evinces an intertextuality within this "empire of signs" (Barthes) that, in the final analysis, frustrates any programmatic determination: "This intertextual relationship is problematic rather than automatic and symmetrical. Any given performance is only to a limited degree constrained by the indications of the written text, just as the latter does not usually bear the traces of any *actual* performance" (Elam 209).

As an example of the type of analysis possible with semiotics, Elam holds up the inordinately complex dramatic calculus for *Macbeth* developed by Etienne Souriau. Composed of lines of symbols or hieroglyphics that purport to translate the action in *Macbeth* into terms common to "200,000 dramatic situations" (a transliteration of the title of Souriau's book on semiotics and theater), the optimism of "a multidisciplinary science . . . united by a common global concern" reaches its apotheosis. Yet Elam distances himself from Souriau's model, as if to express some anxiety about such an extreme semiotics, one that reveals an interesting slippage: "It is by no means clear that this is the appropriate framework in which to consider, say, *Miss Julie* or *Travesties*" (130). Yet it is also at this very point that the dream of a "global concern" itself is suspect. By the time Souriau develops 200,000 dramatic situations, the usefulness of such a model becomes questionable indeed, for, in the proliferation of possibilities, neither change or "play" can take place. Elam fails to address this point adequately. While he finds in the series of interrelated events onstage a tangible understanding of the structure of a theatrical event, he does not recognize the very incompleteness of the event that he suggests will frustrate any formulaic analysis of structure. The gap that produces this failure in Elam's structuralist project is the very one that allows multiple levels to exist at a single point in a text, that is, that disrupts the univocal certainty of meaning. Without a sense of the competing meanings that are present at the surface of language, such as exist in a piece like *Listen to Me*, or of the consequences of the arbitrary relationship between signifier and signified, no understanding of the inherent theatricality of signs is possible.

While starting with similar precepts as Elam, Patrice Pavis finds in semiotics a method for articulating a plurality of signifying systems within the theatrical event that avoids some of Elam's problems. For Pavis, semiology is a possible tool for examining theater practice, one that is not all-encompassing, or transcendental in scope, but, rather, that affords a partial project: "It is . . . productive to . . . examine how the avant-garde uses or disqualifies certain semiotic practices in its creative work" (181). For Pavis, meaning is not fully controllable or fully explicable; it is always belated, always a step behind the production of signs onstage. The inability of the theater's avant-garde (a term, it should be added, that he uses advisedly, given its historical meanings) either to accept traditional structures and trust signs—which always seem to be slipping away from their referents—or to escape those structures and signs altogether makes the avant-garde particularly worthy of analysis, particularly as it continually attempts the latter. Inherent in giving up the traditional codes of stage language is the construction of a system of signage decay:

> Faced with [the] contradiction inherent in any "artistic language" seeking to form a semiological system having its own units and its own specific way of functioning, the avant-garde had to choose between two solutions and two diametrically opposed aesthetics: (1) entirely give up the idea of the sign and the codification of the *mise en scène* or (2) multiply signs and units until the signifying structure degenerates into an infinite series of identical patterns (Pavis 183).

Pavis recognizes the second possibility as most compelling for his analytics, for it points to the loss of the stable relationship between signifier and signified that seems to motivate the event. The avant-garde theater has "lost all confidence in a mimetic reproduction of reality . . . [and] calls into question the mimetic nature of art and the refusal of the stage to presume to imitate a preexistent exterior world" (185).

The primary focus of Pavis's semiological reading of the theater is on the mise-en-scène. For Pavis, the mise-en-scène is important because it can produce a work that generates its own values and affiliations rather than representing an individual ego. Yet, according to Pavis, the contemporary avant-garde theater is in a state of perpetual crisis, for, when it constructs the author of a performance or director as an autonomous subject, able to control completely the mise-en-scène, it replaces one author for another. For example, in his "operas," Robert Wilson creates vast architectures that seem far from the controlling gaze of the "Author-function" and that produce a type of performance more like a landscape of many different theatrical systems of signification (à la Gertrude Stein) than one focused around a written text. Yet in terms of controlling the performance and "authorizing" the images, Wilson remains at the center, that is, remains as the Author who controls and directs the signs onstage: "To replace the structural notion of *mise en scène* by that of an author . . . or director, is thus to fall back into a problematic situation that the avant-garde had indeed resolved to transcend: that of an autonomous subject who is the source of meaning and who controls the totality of signs" (Pavis 182). By undermining the position of the Author as autonomous subject, Pavis imagines an alternative to the "theological stage," which Derrida identifies as the province of author-creators. In this case, the mise-en-scène produces meaning as and in performance according to its construction rather than as the onstage fulfillment of an authorial presence or "theological" intention.

Pavis focuses on the mise-en-scène in order to understand performance that subverts the scene of the father (the word) by raising the possibility of several texts encoded in any onstage moment. In so doing, he begins to ask whether the relationship between word and thing can be trusted. Anne Ubersfeld addresses a similar point by suggesting that the dramatic text is necessarily incomplete until performance. The text contains "holes" that can be covered or completed only through performance, holes that leave in the text a certain openness to interpretation. The insistence, however, on the concept of holes in the text (Ubersfeld) or the "infinite series of identical patterns" (Pavis) implies a closure, a complicated mastery, that raises the question of slippage within the sign. That is, the closure will necessarily be possible, and that it is just a matter of finding a complex enough model to ascertain meaning.

Pavis and Ubersfeld generate an extremely flexible semiology. Yet, at the moment of their greatest complexity, both appear too quick to close the discrepancy that creates the "gap" with a surgical suture ill fitting its implications. While any closure in performance is a tenuous moment of completion at best—that is, whatever meanings assigned are by definition arbitrary and site specific—that it need occur as a defining property of semiology apparently denies the possibility of an uncontrolled breakdown in the particular system's representational codes while harmonizing or unifying meaning at the point at which the system is most in doubt. The problem of closure is significant for both semiotics and structuralism, for even if closure is located in performance, it still suggests that a text can be understood in its entirety and that the incongruities within structure will be resolved as performance. In constructing textual architectures that claim to "survey all the threads" (Derrida), the implications of the margins of theater are avoided in a manner that closes off texts to all but preordained meanings that fit into necessary and unchangeable categories. The blindness in the semiologist's dream of symmetry appears at the point of slippage in the signifier-signified duopoly; it is a blindness, furthermore, that erases competing meanings that may challenge the hegemony of the signifier.

In response to the slippage between signified and signifier Pavis calls for a theater based on "the absence of hierarchy between sign systems, the semiological creativity of the spectator, the part played by chance and event in any theatrical performance" (186). Pavis unifies "what has been only artificially separated: utterance and enunciation, writing and orality, meaning and sound, signifier and signified" by creating a circuit between the unifying aspects of language and the multiplicity of events: "One can only appeal for a semiology that takes all the dimensions of theater into account" (190–91). That is, the semiotician must hope, again, in more complete form, for a transcendental vision that sees the decay of the event as a structural component of the system. The idea of a theater based on the absence of hierarchy between sign systems also begins to sound surprisingly like what Kirby had in mind both for Happenings and for "referentless" theater. By refusing to consider that the differences between sign systems might be significant, Pavis, Kirby, semiotics, and structuralism deny the political status of signs and refuse to account for the theater's institutional affiliations. The value-free theater thus imagined is prey to meanings and systems of signification that may be far from what the individual theorists or practitioners had in mind in their initial escape from traditional "value."

Finally, the very illusion of theater works against the structuralist and semiotic approach, for theatricality is predicated on the "playability" of the gap that appears to be at the very core of dramatic structure. Superimposing a structure upon this indeterminate region, will force the text again into the realm of ontotheological foundations and categories, of philosophies that deny the possibility of an articulate Other. Given that structure and closure are for the most part unavoidable, as Derrida recognizes at the end of his essay on Artaud, what impels a "post-"structuralism is the remembrance that structure can only be contingent and belated if "another thread," another meaning, can appear at any point of performance (or reading).

The disruptive tendency of history to appear onstage as something of a virus that causes the predictable world of structuralism and semiotics to spin wildly out of control is clearly apparent in the work of Heiner Müller. Rather than trying to find a "master-narrative" that will account for all the threads of historical process, for example, Müller contends with fragments that do not necessarily add up to any whole. Müller's *Hamletmachine* confronts the impossibility of the "Hamlet" character in Western drama. While the Shakespearean Hamlet can be read as revealing the impossibility of self-knowledge—or at least of the futility of equating self-knowledge and truth—Müller's Hamlet-machine confronts this futility as a political, historical condition not bound by the strictures of individual ego-psychology.

The actor playing Hamlet:

> I'm not Hamlet. I don't take part any more. My words have noth-
> ing to tell me anymore. My thoughts suck the blood out of the
> images. My drama doesn't happen anymore. Behind me the set is
> put up. By people who aren't interested in my drama, for people
> to whom it means nothing. I'm not interested in it any more either.
> I won't play along. (Müller 1984b, 56)

In the face of historical atrocities, in the recognition of what "Hamlet"
and the construction of a humanist master-narrative means to the
West, "The Actor Playing Hamlet" attempts to reject that role. But it
can not be so easily forsaken, for it is a motor of Western identity.
Thus, Hamlet-machine must live on, after the end of "his" drama,
with the historical consequences of that identity. Müller politicizes
the individual ego in terms of the failures of the West by including
in its fundamental constitution such elements as genocide, totalitari-
anism, and patriarchy:

> In the solitude of airports
> I breathe again I am
> a privileged person. My nausea is a privilege. . . . Somewhere bod-
> ies are torn apart so I can dwell in my shit. Somewhere bodies are
> opened so I can be alone with my blood. My thoughts are lesions
> in my brain. (57)

In Müller's plays, history is neither progressive nor linear. Instead,
it is catastrophic, a nightmare from which there is no awakening
and, more important, no transcendent possibility of understanding
the processes of history as a "pageant" or other "global" narrative.
In his analysis of his own production of some fragments of Müller's
plays, Johannes Birringer recognizes in Müller's despair of either an
individual or collective salvation for the West a crucial failing in the
theater as well:

> If Müller's "Landscape" is the ice-age of . . . defeated illusions, then it is more than likely that the theater cannot but double and magnify the defeat. . . . To stage a deadly language, to bring it alive on . . . stage, then, may not at all help us to see the relationship between the pathos of Müller's murderous vision of defeat and the theatre's own current incapacity to imagine a different reality. (111)

Birringer's pessimism about the theater's ability to comprehend the very historical failings that Müller posits as the inheritance of the West casts doubt on the possibility of ever fully understanding any event, whether in the theater, textual analysis, or politics.

The disappearance of narrative, character, and structure in Müller's plays problematizes theater, for in demanding, for example, that there be absolute congruity between signified and signifier, any sort of random or anarchic occurrences threaten the stability of the system. Yet, without a sense of chance (the "roll of the die" that Gilles Deleuze recognizes as the crux of Nietzsche's eternal return), of incommensurability (what Lyotard calls "the differend"), or of the "parsimonious plurality" (Barthes) that is built into words, no sense of the politics of language (a politics that is, in the first instance, about difference) is possible. In avoiding the equivocation that appears at semiotics' origin (language), the question of history (of origins?) seldom comes up. For example, from where do signs appear? Kirby completely avoids the question. Marvin Carlson proposes that "when we consider semiosis in more general terms . . . we soon come to realize that performance, since it is realized within a culture, can hardly escape [the cultural specificity of signs]" (8). Yet, if as Carlson argues, everything on the stage always already contains certain meanings, despite the artist's intention for the sign, then where do these significations come from? "Semiology does not concern itself with locating meaning . . . but with the mode of production of that meaning throughout the theatrical process" (Pavis 13). If "meaning" is incipient in structure, as appears to be the case given semiotics' silence on the question of history, then all semiotics has accomplished is to shift foundational absolutism from things to words, that is, to give discourse the weight and philosophical privilege formerly reserved for theological origins. Pavis's comment reveals an unproblematized "genesis" of meaning in semiotics. His response to the indeterminacy of the subject in a universe of sliding signage is to construct a system that accounts for slippage *within* it. While Uberfeld's further articulation of a hole between event and structure on which performance is founded complicates the semiotic model, it still seems unable to account for the discursivity of language, for the residuals of power that haunt any knowledge/meaning nexus.

Structuralism's avoidance of what Philippe Lacoue-Labarthe calls historiality limits its usefulness as the "hard science" of the theater world, for it apparently undermines the possibility of an ideological critique. "In the theater that semiology constructs, its imaginary theater, the borders between theater and daily life, aesthetics and sociality, art and ideology, remain impermeable" (Brewer 18). In fact, in numerous books on structuralism, semiotics and theater, history and ideology are either treated as the archiving of artifacts or not treated at all in favor of generating a systematic communicative structure that accounts for as many of the elements of a theatrical performance as possible.[9] In doing so, semiotics has appeared to many of its theater practitioners as an ideal methodology, for it analyzes theater from the assumption that a complete understanding of theater's communicative structure is possible, if difficult. This methodology still avoids the question of what meanings can and do obtain without questioning what Derrida calls the "philosophical intransigence" of the text. In a 1959 essay, written before semiotics and structuralism had actually made many inroads into the theater world, Derrida suggests that there are elements of structure that may not be recognizable to a system that does not interrogate its own foundations: "On the basis of the structural description of a *vision of the world* one can account for everything except the infinite opening to truth, that is, philosophy. Moreover, it is always something like an *opening* which will frustrate the structuralist project. What I can never understand, in a structure, is that by means of which it is not closed" (1978, 160). The "opening" of the structure, the ability of competing interpretations to invade the signifier-signified duopoly, inserts history back into the theater, problematizing the axiomatics of structure.

The "hole" (to turn Ubersfeld's term against her intent) in the "structurality of structure" (Derrida) exists as a theatrics, a mise-en-scène of history that, in its openness, makes impossible a transcendental idealism that might systematize a structure of meaning. This same realization drove Barthes away from his early semiological positions (particularly in *Image-Music-Text* and the *Critical Essays*) to one in which there is less determination, or, for that matter, less chance to master the relationships of signs. As long as semiology keeps sign systems closed, or self-contained, it avoids the problem that interpretation might lie, like the California coastline, on shifting faults or moving sand, or that the concept of structure contains an emphatic ideological function, already coded and marked by specific historical and political apparatus.

It is precisely the destructive, anarchic aspects of historiality that most threaten semiotics' promise of a detached objectivity from which to study sign systems. Without accounting for inexplicable rips in the sociophilosophical fabric of the West, such as the Armenian genocide or the Holocaust, how is it possible to account for the most basic elements of theater, including illusion, except by ignoring history? If hiding and showing define the theatrical moment, then there is something about its structure that has to include its own destruction, not as a terminal event but, instead, as an ongoing process. Consequently, to account for the slippage of the historial in a theatrical text, something other is needed than a system that assigns specific meanings to every object or element, while leaving what it can not contain in a limbolike "hole."

In that it is apparently honor-bound to a world of author-creators and ontotheological textual structures, theater seems perilously at odds with post-structuralist thought. This dismissal, however, ignores the theater's persistent interest in power, in relational dynamics that produce power, rather than in "ontology," or "being," as well as in the apparatus of that very seduction. "Theater places us right at the heart of what is religious-political: in the heart of absence, in negativity, in nihilism as Nietzsche would say, there-fore in the question of power. A theory of theatrical signs, a practice of theatrical signs . . . are based on accepting the nihilism inherent in a representation" (Lyotard 1976, 105). Theater's fascina-tion with power relationships, however disguised in searches for the truth (one of the defining elements of realism), makes it an ideal stage for contemporary theory, for both share this concern with the contingent, historicopolitical foundations of "Being." Much of the post-structuralist displacement of origins starts with the desire to replace philosophy's insistence on ascertaining the nature of an object/concept with an understanding of the mechanics and apparatus that construct objects and concepts as privileged events, with understanding the dynamics of power and, further-more, with recognizing that a number of "discourses," or "phrases," can be operational at any given point. While this state-ment requires a much larger framework in which to explain it, one that I supply throughout the next three chapters, it is worthwhile to note that post-structuralism replaces questions of the ideological status of objects and events with ones of the power dynamics and matrices on which the theorist finds him- or herself operating. As opposed to a more traditional concept of power, politics, and history, Marxist or otherwise, that sees "revolution" only as "the political overthrow from below of one state order and its replace-ment by another" (Anderson 1988, 317), a theater that wishes to be successfully counterhegemonic needs to see power precisely as a "creative force."[10]

In light of the apparent tension arising between the various dis-courses that constitute post-structuralist thought, the "holes" that Ubersfeld suggests will be filled by performance are revealed as on the contrary, radically unfillable and incompatible with the require-ments of unified systems theories. Rather, they resemble what Lyotard calls the differend. The differend exists between two mutu-ally exclusive discourses as a condition that allows some sort of com-munication between the two. He defines the differend as "a case of conflict, between (at least) two parties, that cannot be equitably resolved for lack of a rule of judgement applicable to both arguments. One side's legitimacy does not imply the other's lack of legitimacy" (1988, xi). Lyotard suggests the notion of a differend as a way in which to begin thinking how two discourses—Western metaphysics and "Auschwitz"—that are apparently mutually exclusive (metaphysics asserts the existence of transcendental values; Auschwitz, in Lyotard's reading, asserts the radical contingency of values) could exist in the same historical space. That is, he attempts to enunciate the responsibility of thought in the face of an event that is both the culmination and impossibility of that thought. The differend opens up a discourse of competing phrases that does not, cannot, seek to synthesize (dialectically or otherwise) the competing phrases to a "grand narrative" that functions by suppressing its components into a cohesive unit.

> To give the differend its due is to institute new addresses, new addressers, new significations, and new referents in order that the injustice find an expression and that the plaintiff cease to be a victim. This requires new rules for the formation and linking of phrases. . . . Every injustice must be able to be phrased. It is necessary to find a new competence. (Lyotard 1984, 7)

By attempting to institute new "families of phrases or new genres of discourse" (7) that allow for difference without creating victims, the differend signals the possibility of ending the stalemate that arises from the failure of existing discourses to account for opposing points of view.[11] The usefulness of the differend, it seems, when attempting to balance the various theoretical discourses associated with "deconstruction," is that it neither silences (as an act of domination) nor privileges one "thought" over another, as if there is in fact a master trope ("post-structuralism") on which all others ("feminism," "postcoloniality," "ethnic discourse") are contingent. The differend does not limit the legitimacy of any of these discourses but, instead, maintains their (sometimes fundamental) differences as an active form of exchange.

Once the historial aspect of sign systems is recognized, any sort of closure that might imply a transcendental understanding of a text, event, or performance becomes suspect. This problematic requires that the constituent apparatus of history be considered along with the internal constituents of the text itself. These elements include questions concerning institutions, ideology, power, and, more generally, representation. Maria Minich Brewer sees in the performance of theory that attempts to take into account these sorts of questions a "theatricality [that] can no longer simply be viewed from within a formal, intrinsic understanding of the sign, for each element of the general opposition between signifier and signified, frame and content, inside and outside, is questioned by practices that displace any notion of theatricality as closure" (19). In the breakdown of these oppositions, what good is a system of communication that does not take into account how the components of that system are used to perpetuate the same Platonic hierarchies that have always threatened theater's place in society (and, conversely, that theater itself has threatened)?

> The binary logic of exclusion (either/or) that opposes the presence of theatrical signs to their absent meaning becomes particularly problematic when semiology attempts to account for types of theatre that do not fit into the mold of the classical model of representation. What happens to semiotic oppositions when they are challenged by the most diverse of theatrical practices? (Brewer 19)

For Brewer, they become post-structuralist and, in doing so, reveal that meaning is not a priori fixed between dyadic (Saussure) or triadic (Peirce) sign systems. Rather, meaning may accrue in performance as well as in society on the basis of what is expedient for maintaining dominant social and political structures; conversely, meaning may appear in subversive, counterhegemonic constructions. Either way, the possibility that "meaning" may be at least as important as "structure" in the theater, that what appears onstage may be the workings of power rather than the seamless functioning of an apparatus, suggests that, at some level, the gaps, or *openings*, constituting theatricality are sites wherein the institutional investments of a text appear.

The ideological investments of theater texts can be seen in their institutional investments. In Marsha Norman's *Getting Out*, the apparatus of incarceration pervades the stage space. The play displays a remarkable apparatus: that of the incarceration of the body onstage. The main character, Arlie/Arlene, is always surrounded by what Louis Althusser calls "repressive and ideological state apparatus." The penal system, which confines her with physical and psychological bars in the form of both prisons and jailers; the educational system, which established the limits of her intellectual capacities at an early age; the family, whether in the form of an abusive father and mother or male lovers who literally prostituted her; and the state, which bars her from seeing her child, all combine to circumscribe Arlie/Arlene's life within institutional domains. In fact, these structures themselves have a certain prisonlike quality about them as well, for in the interplay of codes and signs there is an uncomfortable intersection with the institutionality of the theater. It is never established whether Arlie/Arlene is punished for justifiable reasons within the context of the play; what is established, however, is the inevitability of these "incarceral" apparatus being applied to the subject in society either negatively, as in Arlie/Arlene's case, or positively, in the case of those allowed to remain "free":

> The evaluation of an aesthetic and/or a criminal body depends on the interdependence of interpretational codes and disciplinary forces. Any performance of the knowledge and judgement of an institutional body—be it penal or academic—is relational to the performance's power and force, to its ability to delimit interpretation to the scene of its own codes, to its desire to dominate discourse and action which are threatening or indifferent to its own bases of judgmental power. (Murray 1983, 377–78)

Timothy Murray suggests that Foucault's reading of the penal system in *Discipline and Punish* and elsewhere might be a useful first step to approaching institutionality within Norman's play, and within the theater. Furthermore, it suggests that the institution of theater itself is complicit in maintaining the illusion of an unregimented play of signifiers. "Behind the scenes of Norman's theatre, someone is always demanding production and reiterating subjection, always construing orders and making judgement. The offstage placement of this authoritative speech is, moreover, the fundamental element of the economics of the prison" (378). Murray's concern here is to underline the manner in which a particular text—one commonly discussed in terms of its "humanist" qualities—can in fact "perform" the same institutionality as it portrays diegetically. Norman's text performs a remarkable reinforcement of patriarchal institutionality, one that conceals how the "free play" of signifiers (that make up "Subject Holsclaw's" world) depends in fact on an authoritarian apparatus that disperses "freedom" according to what serves its (ideological) interests.[12]

If the power of the institution depends on the absence of its source of authority, the theater, with its absent author-creators (Derrida) that busily disseminate power discourses, could easily seem like a prison house. The laws or systems that structure meaning are themselves based upon a conceit that is constructed in a particular social, political, and, therefore, historical scene. This reversal of the structuralist paradigm—"a system of differences without positive terms" (Saussure)—invokes a slippage between the signified and signifier in the first instance and suggests that any such slippage is contained by ideology, given that it is impossible to imagine a language that does not weigh various signs differently.

Yet, regardless of internal structure, how is a text ideological? By ideological, I do not mean the configuration suggested in popular media of "ideologies" that are somehow held and disseminated by a few evil men nor a model of thought consciously assumed by a transhistorical individual. Instead, ideology composes and generates, according to Althusser, "not the system of the real relations which govern the existence of individuals, but the imaginary relation of those individuals to the real conditions in which they 'live'" (1971, 169). Althusser recognizes that the interpellation of a subject into ideology (the mirror phase in which the subject becomes a subject by both differentiating and identifying with an image of him- or herself in language) is a performance that takes place at "the site of a competition and a struggle in which the sound and fury of humanity's political and social struggles is faintly or sharply echoed" (Althusser 1969, 149n). The struggle at this site configures ideology as an ongoing process.

As such, every performance of this sort takes place within a political realm, regardless of what formal or personal structures are apparent. "We can see that the play itself *is* the spectator's consciousness—for the essential reason that the spectator has no other consciousness than the content which unites him to the play in advance, and the development of this content in the play itself: the new result which the play *produces* from the self-recognition whose image and presence it is" (151). In a certain sense, ideology is a form of theater (and theater a form of ideology) that first forms and is formed at the level of language and that precedes and anticipates the subject. For Althusser, ideology is a condition, if not a definition, of language; thus, the individual is "hailed" by ideology when it enters language, that is, when it becomes a subject. As the subject constructs a relationship to his or her "real conditions of existence" by experiencing and representing those conditions through language, subjectivity obtains as a product of the recognition (the mirror phase) of selfhood in language.

This process has immediate implications for the theater. "What we recognize as credible in performance is more often than not what we have come to accept as credible in that closed circle of the ideological which . . . produces not perception and knowledge . . . but the confirmation of what we already know and believe" (Blau 1983, 458). The disturbing coincidence of ideology and performance, as both Althusser and Blau recognize, suggests that what might naively be considered as "truth" within a text (the New Critical moment) is in fact based upon a language that speaks discursively, not transcendentally, a language that constitutes the subject as an effect of power.

Althusser's reworking of Lacan and Marxism is useful to rehearse for it suggests that the subject is constructed and maintained as/at a nexus of culturally determined and determining forces. This conception of ideology makes clear the link between knowledge, truth, and power. According to Mohammad Kowsar, "In Althusser's design art and art criticism (aspects of ideological activity) function as necessary 'systems of representations' in context of the relative autonomy of ideology itself" (464). The problem of what constitutes knowledge offers, in accordance with Althusser's Marxist intentions, a prime opportunity for ascertaining the role of history in the text and textuality: "Ideology is not an aberration or a contingent excrescence of history; it is a structure essential to the historical life of societies. Further, only the existence and the recognition of its necessity enable us to act on ideology and transform ideology into an instrument of deliberate action on history" (Althusser 1969, 232). That ideology needs a subject makes apparent that it cannot simply be tossed off in pursuit of "the truth" but, rather, that it is an indelible condition of life. This reversal of the cogito has had a remarkable influence on contemporary theory.[13]

While Althusser's formulation of ideology is a useful entry point into history, it is problematic, for it does not necessarily succeed as a universal model. Teresa de Lauretis suggests that Althusser's notion of ideology, despite its attention to the complicity of the entire social order in constructing the representational apparatus that inculcates subjectivity within dominant ideology, is incomplete or inadequate, in that it denies, elides, or ignores the actual effects of gender. In her essay "The Technology of Gender" she proposes a possible alternative to Althusser's formula that "all ideology has the function (which defines it) of 'constituting' concrete individuals as subjects" (Althusser 1971, 171). By substituting *gender* for *ideology*, the formula holds, but in different form: "Gender has the function (which defines it) of 'constituting' concrete individuals as men and women. That shift is precisely where the relation of gender to ideology can be seen, and seen to be an effect of the ideology of gender" (de Lauretis 1987, 6). de Lauretis intimates that there is more at stake in recognizing the effects of ideology than discovering "the actions of history." Her analysis makes apparent the struggle that always constitutes representation-in/as-ideology. This struggle directly affects the constitution of gendered subjects in a society in which one side of the gender equation is always (already) under erasure: "To deny gender, first of all, is to deny the social relations of gender that constitute and validate the sexual oppression of women; and second, to deny gender is to remain 'in ideology'" (15). The subject is not simply a subject but is also gendered and racially identified—both instances that work against the notion that meaning can be held only within the written, literary, text, that meaning might be universal, or that a text can hide from the textuality that constitutes difference. While Althusser analyzes how ideology invades and constitutes the subject, de Lauretis shows how the subject is not a universal position but is constituted by and through difference. In fact, for de Lauretis, Althusser's subject-in-ideology is specifically coded as male, for the recognition game in the mirror phase in which the subject is "hailed" by ideology constitutes *her* as object for the male subject.[14]

Indeed, even de Lauretis's rereading of Althusser is susceptible to a similar critique, for, in reading *gender* in the place of *ideology*, de Lauretis apparently overlooks other areas in which her critique could apply. Certainly *race, age, physical disability*, or *class* could be substituted for *gender* in this equation, with as powerful implications. It seems strange that de Lauretis would want to make a simple binary substitution at such a contestable space: that of the constitution of the subject in dominant discourse.[15] Ideology is not a monolith inherited perforce by the arrival of language, nor is it a set of beliefs adopted by a Cartesian cogito. Instead, it is, as Althusser maintains, a struggle to perpetuate certain productions of meaning and the apparatus to support them. Ideology does not function in the same way for all of its constituents; any sense of a universalizing tendency in ideology must be resisted in favor of the interrelation of ideology and specific discursive practices (e.g., racism, ageism, homophobia) within a given cultural location.

At issue in discerning the ideological underpinnings of texts is, among other things, the question of representation, of how certain things, events, or people are represented, of what is represented, and, furthermore, of what can be made of the images that most commonly appear and reappear onstage. In fact, the very notion of periodization in theater history has come under intense scrutiny recently:

> [Dominant history is] Whig history, written by the victors, or at least by the victors of the moment. In such texts historical instances featuring the "right" answers predominate massively over the "wrong" ones, even if the latter were by far the more important to contemporaries. Such procedures . . . make for wildly distorted history. (Roach 15)

In *The Player's Passion*, Joseph Roach describes a method that attempts to see acting theory outside of the perspective of modern acting theories but without denying that any perspective is inexorably marked with the individual writer's historial position. Roach's study of the history of acting suggests that there is always an issue in historical analysis concerning the validity of "what really happened" and, furthermore, that it may be impossible to judge a historical period from any objective criteria without at least considering the possibility that that very criteria may itself be historically marked. In similar manner, Thomas Postlewait intimates that the writing of history might be as complex an event as following writing out to the "margins" of the text, when he writes that,

> despite our commitment to accurate documentation, description, and analysis, our access to the historical event is always problematic. . . . Historical study, which by definition presupposes a reality outside of subjective consciousness and systems of discourse, must challenge any assumption that all explanations are equally sufficient or appropriate. (162)

The problem of certainty in interpreting historical texts is not solved simply because the particular text seems to contain "factual," or objective, information within it. "Every event is open to a number of descriptions, each of which offers a partial perspective—but not a complete and final description" (162). Not only is interpretation clouded by the problem that no one source can stand in for an entire epoch, but the question of whose version of the story is remembered must always be accounted for.[16]

In *Theatrical Legitimation: Allegories of Genius in Seventeenth-Century England and France*, Timothy Murray suggests, however, that the "new historicism" also has limitations. While new historicism has certainly expanded the historical canon to include the cultural and economic conditions of peoples underrepresented in "standard histories," it has not been as attentive to the ideological context and conditions of the texts analyzed and created. "In its differing quests for sociological reconstruction, the 'new historicism' must defer rigorous critique of the psycho-epistemological filament sustaining the differing expressions of confidence in critical mastery" (Murray 1987, 5). Such study ends up replicating the ideological structures at work in the texts reconstructed, for it does not, by itself, offer a methodology for analyzing the institutional apparatus by which a text is produced: "Much of this scholarship reasserts, for example, the force of the traditional 'master-narrative' by analyzing how texts generate singular, 'master' discourses" (4). Instead, Murray argues, both the text and the epistemological structures and institutions of the text must constantly be considered when writing history. "At stake is less the discovery of 'new histories' than the re-presentation of familiar methodologies, less an aesthetic appreciation of the aspects in which historical artifacts offer themselves than a theoretical deconstruction of the epistemological structures shaping historical narrative" (6). To this end, Murray utilizes a wide range of post-structuralist and deconstructionist texts to analyze how a coterie of "genius" writers and readers was instrumental to the appearance of legitimate and illegitimate modes of discourse and, furthermore, what particular institutional or structural psychoepistemological apparatus of the period allowed the production of such texts.[17]

The usefulness of approaching history as a series of discourses competing for ideological dominance has proven particularly useful to feminist writers. In particular, the need to escape standard interpretations and stories in the theater has led many women to provide texts that are not indebted to the aesthetic in canonical drama that provides only subservient roles for women, regardless of the amount of "universal suffering" they contain. The innocence of theater as cultural production disappears, in Hélène Cixous's view, with her recognition that it "is built according to the dictates of male fantasy, [and] repeats and intensifies the horror of the murder scene which is at the origin of all cultural productions" (1984, 546). Once the underlying ideological assumptions that motivate and drive textual coherency and narrative resolution are revealed, the authority with which these practices imbue a text becomes less certain. Cixous asks, "How, as women, can we go to the theatre without lending our complicity to the sadism directed against women, or being asked to assume, in the patriarchal family that the theatre reproduces *ad infinitum*, the position of victim?" (546). Yet Cixous begins to think against the classical theater's misogyny and consequently opens the question of marginalities on the stage. In imagining the stage as a woman's place, she begins to reinvent history, to raise the question, again, of what constitutes history: "It is a different Story. It will be a text, a body decoding and naming itself in one long, slow push" (547). That most cultural production requires the "murder of woman" impels Cixous to articulate a sensibility that disrupts the apparent congruity between representation and its "objects," actual lived experience, in order to counter dominant ideology.

Similarly, Josette Féral pursues the disassembly of theatrical systems incipient upon a "master's language" by imagining a stage discourse of "non-mastery, in which the subject rejects the criteria of correct syntax and opts for incorrectness and errors as a sign of her own marginality and uncenteredness." The gaps that appear in place of a smooth, complete surface undermine the author-function by revealing spaces that both threaten and liberate theatrical economies: "In the gaps and repetitions, modifications, suspension points of an unfinished sentence and exclamation points that signpost the text are revealed the hesitations of a speaker" (560). The political charge given this line of textual de(con)struction from feminism provides the patternings of an alternative practice as well as the tools to understand the unseemly consequences of textual mastery as a philosophical strategy.

Cixous is a crucial figure in post-structuralist theater, for she writes both theoretical and dramatic texts. In *Portrait of Dora*, Cixous restages the sessions of one of Freud's most famous patients, Dora, as a refusal of psychoanalytic incarceration. In the play, Dora is being analyzed by Freud in order to find a cure for her "overactive" sexual imagination. Dora is attracted to Mrs. K., a mother figure in the play. Freud will not recognize this as a possible sexual attachment but only as the sublimation of the actual desire for Mr. K., the missing father, in fulfillment of the Electra complex. Freud's persistent misreading of the situation earns Dora's growing ridicule, until finally she rejects him and leaves. The play suggests that Freud, in ascribing Dora's affections to an Electra complex, is actually transferring his own desire onto Dora, reading himself in the guise of her therapy.

In rejecting a psychoanalytic master-narrative, the play also rejects linear time. Scenes between Freud and Dora and scenes with characters from her past appear together onstage, allowing Dora's desire to be diffuse and multiple. Rosette Lamont sees the play as a vehicle in which the desire for freedom from the law of the father is expressed: "In her simultaneously lyric and tragic text, Cixous transmits Dora's gasp for breath. The whole work is a cry of pain, a repressed sob. And yet, in the end, we witness the young woman's triumph and the scientists' discomfort" (88). Her understanding of both Freud's actual case and Cixous's plays as a confirmation of woman's escape from her role in patriarchal society ("On the reverse side of Dora's portrait, we find the face of all her sisters, oppressed for many centuries but finally clearing a path towards freedom" [92]) is based on Dora's ability to imagine herself as whole, to dream of herself as an agent of change. Simone Benmussa, who helped develop the script, makes a connection between the stage and dreams: "In 'stage work,' just as in 'dream work,' a situation, or a desire, is projected into space by a word or a gesture: stage work produces images. Stage is the reflecting surface of a dream, of a deferred dream, it is the meeting place of the desires. . . [that] create around them a nebulous zone which allows the spectator to divine the other" (9). Through the simultaneity and multiplicity of images onstage, the Other is able to appear, momentarily freed from structures that allow only one possibility to appear at any point onstage or in a text.

At the same time, however, the efficacy of this appearance of the Other in Cixous's text is questionable from a political point of view, for, in leaving Freud, Dora remains isolated. In her reading of *Portrait of Dora*, Jeannette Savona suggests that this isolation is finally crippling to Dora, despite her apparent freedom at the end of the play: "In *Portrait* . . . we are presented with an apolitical female oasis which remains marginal and inefficient. . . . [Dora] remains the prisoner of her solitude, despite her final departure." In this case, the dream work remains within the confines of the social structures it attempts to transcend because it does not form a link to a world beyond solitary reflection: "*Portrait* reflects . . . the difficulty of creating a new form of feminist theater within institutions founded on both the division and repression of women" (105). Inherent in the creation of an individual subject, then, are the same confining structures and traits that led to Dora's initial incarceration.

The Platonic hierarchy of increasingly true representations that gain value and legitimacy as they approach the status of the Same implies a (necessarily) incomplete quest for truth. "Realism's fetishistic attachment to the true referent and the spectator's invitation to rapturous identification with a fictional imago serve the ideological function of mystifying the means of material production, thereby concealing historical contradictions, while reaffirming or mirroring the 'truth' of the status quo" (Diamond 1989b, 5). In constructing a feminist mimesis in the theater, Elin Diamond describes a text that breaks with traditional realist structures. Rather than remaining organized around a single transcendental principle, this text is attuned to and includes a multitude of meanings and possibilities. In realism's place, Diamond imagines (with the help of Julia Kristeva and Luce Irigaray) a form of mimesis that eschews the Platonic hierarchy of meanings and representations attendant on a phallogocentric economy's truth-effect. In Irigaray's restaging of the cave metaphor as metonymy, Diamond finds a "'mimetic system' that completely belies the model-copy, for to the prisoners [in the cave] no origin of the image projections is imaginable; or, to put it another way, what they experience as origin is always already mimicry, a representation of repetition" (10). Mimicry disables the very possibility of conforming to a philosophically defined Same, for it throws into question the legitimacy of the relationship between signified and signifier.

Caryl Churchill's *A Mouthful of Birds* demonstrates some of the narrative disruptions that Diamond suggests would open in the theater as a space of free play. In the play, seven characters are gradually overcome by passion in such a way that they lose their specifically designated social roles. The character Derek's body is inhabited by Pentheus and is torn apart, as in the *Bacchae*. Even though he is torn up here, it is not simply a matter of repeating the Greek play, for Derek/Pentheus creates a transsexual identity out of the ruins of the rigorously gendered body. "My breasts aren't big but I like them. My waist isn't small but it makes me smile. My shoulders are still strong. . . . My skin used to wrap me up, now it lets the world in. . . . Every day I wake up, I'm comfortable" (Churchill 71). The potential for misidentification of the transsexual Derek/Pentheus undermines the normative codes that formulate the gendered body, for this "two-way" body does not subscribe to the either/or of gender. As a result, this body "ruins representation. It undermines a patriarchy that disciplines the body into gender opposition; it dismantles the phallomorphic economy that denies visibility to the female" (Diamond 1989a, 277). In place of the search for Truth that motivated Plato's cave metaphor, an unruly, theatrical clamor resides parasitically on the residuals of Truth, mocking and dismantling them. Diamond's reading of mimesis in the context of bodies that are not recognizable within the domain of normative discourse (such as appear in *A Mouthful of Birds*) opens possibilities in representation that simply do not assume the burdensome cloak of realism. This mimesis, furthermore, is attentive to gender constructions and differences. The play of differences is essential to the entire notion of theater, which "is also, and in a complex sense, the place of play, and unlike other media, in the theatre the same play—and the 'Same' theory—can be played not only again, but differently" (Diamond 1989b, 20).

By problematizing transhistorical or transcendental structures of "meaning," feminist theater makes clear its ideological heritage and nature. Feminist theater is, however, certainly not the only one to make the search for alternative stage spaces and counterhegemonic texts of central importance. Similar claims can be made for ethnic theaters, including, among others, those of African American, Asian American, and Mexican American writers and practitioners and for gay and lesbian theaters. Furthermore, because these groups can be associated with a critique of authoritarian apparatus and institutions in theater and society does not mean that they can be conveniently lumped together on the periphery of theatrical enterprises. What these groups do share is an interest in the margin as a site that constructs and unravels meaning as a hegemonic institution. I have emphasized feminist concerns in this section not in order to establish feminism as the master trope of difference but because I return to the issues of race and sexual preference in chapters 4 and 5. It is important to note that an awareness of the ideological function and status of institutions pervades the theory and theater texts that I use in this project, and it is impossible to privilege one particular set of texts or sensibilities (whether they be post-structuralist, feminist, or otherwise).

The post-structuralist turn in critical discourse, along with feminism, post-coloniality, and ethnic discourse, has moved the question of difference to center stage. The differing dynamics of age difference, gender difference, racial difference, and class difference (not that all are equivalent) are of critical importance to understanding contemporary discourse. Traditionally, either sexual or racial difference has been used to support a simple, biologically based and biased binary division. Thus naturalized through reference to biology, difference is used as a safeguard to maintain and uphold notions of Truth, Value, and Beauty by providing a simple analogic Other that can be invoked to quell any threat to a system of purity and privilege. The specific mechanisms of these structures are so well analyzed elsewhere that it would be redundant to rehearse them again here. Suffice to say, however, that the traditional sense of difference, based on biology and manifested through binary, exclusionary structures, has been attacked from many corners in contemporary discourse. If these structures still exist, however, it is not through lack of effort by their critics but, rather, is a reminder of the depth to which ageism, racism, sexism, and homophobia penetrate, and, for that matter, structure and define Western thought.

The debate concerning the canon appears in two very different forms in the theory and theater texts that I use in the following chapters. On the one hand, post-structuralist theory has worked very hard to provide detailed theoretical blueprints for ways of thinking alternative to those that created the Western canon(s)—for example, Gilles Deleuze and Félix Guattari in *A Thousand Plateaus* and Luce Irigaray in *L'Oubli de l'air chez Martin Heidegger*. On the other hand, critique of the Western tradition while remaining within it is the basis of "deconstruction." Derrida's major figures for analysis include Plato, Hegel, Rousseau, and Husserl, among others; Deleuze and Guattari derive "schizoanalysis" from their earlier critique of Freud, Lacan, and Marx, and Irigaray reads Heidegger with a critical intensity similar to that of Derrida (albeit with different investments and outcomes). In a similar manner, the playtexts of which I provide close readings in the next three chapters both model a new awareness of their "margins" and remain within the framework of traditional narrative theater. While they are sensitive to the requirements for a textual practice that, by keeping as many "threads" in play as possible, opens the stage to the full possibilities of theatricality, rather than limiting it to evaluation in terms of meaning, they also simply tell a story of one sort or another. In much the same way as post-structuralist theory retains a connection to what it deconstructs, this theater contains remnants of the theater of the "well-made play."

It is the very complexity of the mode of thinking that has come to be known as "post-structural" that makes it so useful in articulating the margins of theater and the theater at the margins. These theater texts do not actually constitute a new canon or a new ideal for what the theater should be. What Derrida shows, through deconstruction, is that there is a theater at the margins of textuality, that the margin is where words both hide and show their meanings, their possibilities. The theatricality of this process, then, this hiding and showing that is part of the process of deferring and "differing" (i.e., differentiating) meaning (*différance*), allows the greatest number of possibilities on the stage. Consequently, when this *différance* is expanded to include political and social as well as linguistic concerns, the poststructured stage is born.

CHAPTER 2

Phantoms of Theater: Closure in the Plays of Richard Foreman and Rainer Werner Fassbinder

There is always a surprise in store for the anatomy or physiology of any criticism that might think it had mastered the game, surveyed all the threads at once, deluding itself, too, in wanting to look at the text without touching it, without laying a hand on the "object," without risking—which is the only chance of entering into the game, by getting a few fingers caught—the addition of some new thread.

—Jacques Derrida, *Dissemination*

There is a vast difference between destroying in order to conserve and perpetuate the established order of representations, models and copies, and destroying the models and copies in order to institute the chaos which creates, making the simulacra function and raising a phantasm—the most innocent of all destructions, the destruction of Platonism.

—Gilles Deleuze, *The Logic of Sense*

The German playwright and filmmaker Rainer Werner Fassbinder and the U.S. theater *auteur* Richard Foreman have written numerous texts for the theater that pursue ideas of great interest to post-structuralism, texts whose philosophical projects can be viewed as "a continuation of theory by other means," to paraphrase Pierre Clausewitz's dictum on war ("War is the continuation of politics by other means"). Foreman's Ontological Hysteric Theatre pieces continuously attempt to create an event wherein the audience becomes aware of the mechanisms of perception and of the ontological nature of the stage. By enunciating the hysteria that lies below representation, Foreman forces the stage to account for its own ontotheological status, one that traditional theater is invested in denying, for it constitutes at some level a threat to the "well-made play." Foreman's texts need to be read in the context of the theater's ontological condition because they represent a unique concern with form and rhetoric that is intended to call into question the foundational structures of the theater, and to explore the means by which meaning is produced

43

in theater. At the same time, Foreman's plays, especially the ones from the 1970s, are in a sense hermetically complete events, and to consider his written texts in isolation (texts that could be only problematically reproduced by "not-Foreman") is to a degree to give short shrift to the entirety of his work. This danger always arises in talking about theater outside of performance, but it is not in any case my intention to complete a "final dossier" on Foreman.

In the United States, Fassbinder is best known for his films, yet he began his artistic career in the theater. Over the course of ten years, Fassbinder wrote approximately ten plays, five of which have been translated into English, directed numerous productions, and served briefly as the artistic director for Frankfurt's Theater am Türn. Unlike other German playwrights such as Peter Handke, Heiner Müller, and Peter Weiss, Fassbinder's plays have not been given major productions in the United States. The obscurity of his plays in this country is an oversight, however, for they advance a textual form that incorporates a historical understanding with a theoretical critique of such mechanisms as narrative, character development, closure, and the teleological project of Western drama. Furthermore, neither history nor theory acts as an appendage to an already formed textuality; rather, history and theory play integral roles in the creation of Fassbinder's literary and philosophical modes.

Together, then, Foreman's and Fassbinder's plays embody a line of thought that could be called deconstructive, yet the intent and aims of their textual practices differ widely. Foreman's texts raise the stakes on "the closure of representation" by confronting the stage with the consequences of its reliance on traditional economies. Fassbinder apparently has no patience with these economies. Instead, his texts so overcode the theater's constituent elements that they become hyperreal and, in doing so, reveal the fundamental simulation behind representational structures.

Richard Foreman's plays are exemplary of the critical attention currently being paid to the position and forms of authority that structure and motivate textual systems. The questions of where, how, and to what end the mechanics that structure texts according to a hierarchical, or "theological," economy are also central to Derrida's work, in particular his essay "The Theatre of Cruelty and the Closure of Representation." By placing Foreman's and Derrida's textual systems in close proximity, I hope to explore some of the metaphysical mechanisms of Foreman's texts in the context of recent critical studies.

In his writings and stagings Foreman continually asks what constitutes representation and how it functions onstage: "I try to get into the greatest difficulty possible. Syntactically, logically, rationally, narratively. 'Train-of-thought' trouble and blockage is cultivated. The center of the work is in that trouble, stumbling, drift, in that resistance to all 'effort'" (Foreman 1985, 193). From his earliest work in the late 1960s with the Ontological Hysteric Theatre to his recent productions, Foreman has been fascinated with the problems of representation, with creating a stage experience that draws attention to its own ontological status even as it proceeds to create a representational stage space: "Remember that structure is always a combination of the THING and the PERCEIVING of it" (222). His fascination with looking into, and around, rather than just at things, along with his desire to force the image to fall apart in preset patterns, has led him into experimentations with character, space, and text in order to establish some sort of groundwork on which to build an "antitheological" representation.

To a certain degree, Foreman's specular emphasis comes out of his background with a New York "avant-garde" film community called The Group in the 1960s. The members of this group, which included Jonas Mekas, Stan Brakhage, Shirley Clarke, Emile de Antonio, Edward Bland, and Lewis Allen, among others, were concerned with the film as a tactile, physical event as much as a transparent medium. While their practices were immensely varied, they shared a disregard for the "well-made" narrative product. Both P. Adam Sitney and Patricia Mellencamp, among others, perform more rigorous readings of these filmmakers than is possible here, though, it can be said, at the risk of overgeneralization, that this group's primary focus was on the formal qualities of cinema.[1] Departing sharply from the classic realist cinema's reliance on narrative and representation, they focused on structure and perception. In Michael Snow's *Wavelength*, for example, a camera at one end of a loft is set on auto-zoom and focused on the window opposite it. Forty-five minutes later, the zoom, and the film, are complete when the camera focuses on a picture of the sea at the other end of the loft. During this excruciating period, the only "action" is four random human events, including a death, which take place off-camera. The zoom is accompanied by actual ambient sounds during the four events as well as a continuous electronic sound that increases from 50 to 12,000 cycles per second after forty minutes.[2] In place of a narrative, the room itself and the field of vision take on their own lives: what normally occur as background and scenery take on importance far beyond what a quick glance would give them, redefining, in the space of the zoom, the spatiotemporal relationship of object and event. In similar manner, Stan Brakhage's *The Text of Light* ups the ante on perception by filming for fifteen minutes through a glass ashtray. Events and motion are reflected as pure light in this film, an effect that proceeds, as the film progresses, to establish its own logic according to the structural composition of light.[3] The perceptual world that these filmmakers challenged is duplicated in Foreman's assault on the ontological realm that, at least for Foreman, describes the theater world. These films' antipsychologism finds further reflection in Foreman's texts, for he constantly battles the temptation to pander to sentimental conventions of character and affect.

It is interesting that Foreman acknowledges his greatest intellectual debt not to film but, rather, to Gertrude Stein. Stein's concern is to make language resonate outside its conventional boundaries, to foreground the plastic elements of words in order to construct them as objects that escape the simplicity of language-as-medium. One example of this is Stein's phrase that "a rose is a rose is a rose," in which she implodes object (a rose), word (a rose), and concept/ideal (a rose) through their proximal repetition into an artifact that exists without displacement—that is, without the word filling in for something that is presumed absent—in a continuous present. For Stein, the idea of a continuous present, or perceptually pure moment, was central to her formation of a literary phenomonology. In *The Geographical History of America or the Relation of Human Nature to the Human Mind*, she separates the human mind, or being, from human nature, or existence. The value accorded "being" is that it provides an eternal, organic relation to itself that implies a purity of self-knowledge, a prelapsarian state that allows knowledge to escape the mere associative understandings that come from knowing something only through its relationship to other things.

Stein attempted to create a pure perceptual experience through her writing. By doing so, she hoped to alleviate "syncopation," a condition wherein the audience is always one step behind the action onstage, for it never quite has as much knowledge as the characters onstage, that is, is always receiving a narrative after the fact. In writing "landscape plays" that did not depend on the remembrance of previous events, Stein placed moments side by side onstage, moments that were to be experienced in and of themselves, as a continuous flow of presence.[4]

In his Ontological Hysteric Manifestos, Foreman follows Stein's insistence on the importance of apperception: "The result of being awake (seeing). . . [is] you see. You see yourself seeing. . . [and] learn how to be in two places (levels, orientations, perspectives) at once" (Foreman 1976, 143). The mirror metaphor of the doubling process wherein the cogito recognizes its Other and the consequences of staging this displacement of being are not lost on Foreman, for, at the same time he asks his audience to watch itself, his characters onstage consciously construct themselves as constructions. His theater constantly creates positions for watching oneself watch a performance. In Foreman's work, there is always some sense that the "real" event does not take place onstage, nor behind what is onstage, but exists somewhere between the perception of the event and the event itself. What Foreman seeks to create for his audience is in part a replication of his mind. "The actors, then, serve as blank faces on which Foreman sketches aspects of his 'being-in-the-world'; they are representatives of figures of his inner life" (Marranca 4). By recognizing itself in the stage space as if for the first time, the audience will be drawn into an encounter with its own relationship to language. "The word profound must be replaced, so that we no longer follow its lead in thinking that the ultimate is a matter of 'depth'—but come to understand it as a matter of wideness" (Foreman 1985, 191). Simultaneously, the audience will be able to develop an understanding of the ontological consequences of its participation in the illusion of representation through a foregrounding of the theater of language, which, for Foreman, is structured like a film. Ideally, in the "cinematic reproduction of the human mind" (Sitney 191) the audience will see both the object and its implications, a ruse Foreman invents for forestalling the hysteria normally encountered within representation. "Within [the new ontological mode of theater] hysteria lies as a seed/spark which forces the unseeable to cast shadows" (Foreman 1976, 70). Through the revelation and exploration of hysteria, then, Foreman attempts to account for the processes of representation.

Pandering to the Masses: A Misrepresentation creates a "continuous present," a sense of the world that does not refer to a series of remembered, narrativized events but, rather, that constructs an "eternal now" of phenomenological presence. The two main characters, Max and Rhoda, are on quests, the one for worldly experience, the other for knowledge. Narrative illusion manifests in the play through the "Voice," an offstage taped "character" who enters into discussions with the other characters and adds omniscient commentary. The "illusion" that the Voice provides, however, is highly problematic, for at every turn the voice comments as much on its own statements as on the narrative itself. In fact, because of its circularity, it is perhaps a misnomer to identify the narrative as such, if narrative implies a progression. Instead, *Pandering to the Masses* presents onstage the circuity of thought, calling to attention the very thought processes that create narrative in the first place.

The Voice frames the play's participation within the system of ontotheological representation. By commenting throughout the play, this device divides the piece into prologue, beginning, and various sections, each of which stands as a coherent whole. The Voice's comments often serve as direct guides within the representational space of each scene:

Voice: Ladies and gentlemen. This play, at its center, tells of Rhoda, who is still off stage, and her introduction into a secret society, which dispenses a very particular kind of knowledge, which Rhoda learns to endure, which Max, who sits up center, learns to think about. This knowledge has to do with energy, effort, difficulty, awkwardness, failure, and then, effort renewed. (Foreman 1977, 15)

The knowledge to which Rhoda is introduced involves understanding the nature of objects:

> *Voice:* Sophia, Eleanor, and the not yet fully initiated Rhoda, turn their attention back to subjects not yet fully resolved, such as leaf: fragrance: nose: knowing: thinking.
> *Eleanor:* Put the leaf under my nose.
> *Ben:* I see. I see.
> *Rhoda, Sophia, Eleanor:* Ahhhhhhh!
> *Ben:* Nobody has yet thought that knowledge could enter through the nose. You understand. People have said . . . knowledge could come through the ear, through the eye, even through the mouth. . . . But nobody has said, "ah yes, through the nose."
> *Rhoda:* Didn't you remember.
> *Ben:* What.
> *Rhoda:* Didn't it occur to you that maybe I was
> *Ben:* What.
> *Rhoda:* Smelling. The letter. (26)

Rhoda is introduced to several concepts pertaining to perception throughout the play, in order to help her make sense of the world. Her counterpart, Max, has knowledge; Rhoda must struggle through a strange set of interludes toward the discovery of truth. Along the way, it is not certain exactly what the other characters are doing in any psychologically motivated sense. Instead of existing as individuals, they present Rhoda with a number of logical paradoxes or situational dilemmas that she must solve. When a python appears quite unexpectedly and Rhoda is enwrapped in it, Rhoda must consider what about the snake gives it its unique "snakeness," a situation further complicated by the snake's apparent death halfway through the scene. Rhoda's ultimate realization from this and other events is of the necessity of "Proof" (36), or the perceptual confirmation of knowledge.

After Rhoda arrives at "Proof" as the key to knowledge, the Voice dictates the end of the play. It also adds, however, a curious account of the play's philosophical groundwork:

> *Voice:* The play is over. But the meaning of the play will be found within the pages of the books scattered across the floor. Such works including: *The Phenomenology of the Spirit* by Frederich Hegel; *The Cartesian Meditations* by Edmund Hauptfriel; *The Introduction to Logic and Aesthetics* by Morris Shlicksberg; and, of course the text of *Pandering to the Masses: A Misrepresentation.* (36)

The last phrase: "the meaning of the play will be found within. . . the text of *Pandering to the Masses: A Misrepresentation* " is of particular interest. If such a statement implies that meaning is self-consciously constructed within the text, as opposed to being constructed through the text by association with an external order (an arrangement that Foreman borrows from Stein), then what sort of shift of perspective is taking place within the space of that text?

> *Voice:* Try looking through the wrong end of the telescope. Everything looks sharper, doesn't it? (16)

In traditional textuality, founded on such transcendental notions as the Cartesian cogito or Hegelian *Aufhoben*, the text itself is seen as only a conduit by which to perceive the external order that corresponds to, reflects, and creates that text. Consequently, the mechanisms of textuality are themselves concealed so as not to distract from the experience of the particular external order addressed by the text. In *Pandering to the Masses*, however, Foreman draws attention to both the external representational order and to its textual processes by inserting the taped voice as a conspicuous extradiegetic device that interrupts and directs the characters' drama. Throughout the text, the Voice is there to organize events and draw attention to what it considers particularly relevant in any scene. By placing the text of *Pandering to the Masses* in with its own philosophical foundations—in this case three defining texts of the Western tradition—Foreman forces those foundations back to the surface of the text. In doing so, he argues that the most profound moment of understanding is the understanding of a thing in itself, a phenomenologically pure moment of self-recognition akin to what Rhoda realizes after her episode with the snake.

Yet Foreman's gesture toward the Steinian ontological complexity of including the text itself in a diegetic reference to other texts (*The Phenomenology of the Spirit*, e.g.) is not simply an homage. While the three books mentioned appear to be standard works on phenomenology and philosophy, Foreman gets the actual names of Friedrich Hegel, Edmund Husserl, and Moritz Schlick and their books "wrong"; that is, he throws an ironic spin on phenomenology in the form of the misidentified authors. If one of phenomenology's projects is to define rigorously the distinctions between words and objects, to create a contingent certainty based not on philosophical abstractions or teleologies but, rather, on the perceptual world as defined through language, then this misidentification is perhaps the cruelest joke that can be played on phenomenology. Without certainty, what meanings are possible?[5]

Foreman's joke at the expense of philosophy raises serious problems for the theological imperatives behind the space of representation, problems that threaten phenomenology's well-ordered foundations. The "theological stage" is grounded in metaphysical nonpresence in order successfully to play out its economy of representation (Derrida 1978). In this system, the thing represented, the object or authority that structures the binomial sign, can never be present. In its absence, however, a systematized territory of substitutes can be formed to replace it. The play within this string of substitutes constitutes the field or terrain of representation, forming a constant web of signification over the empty space of the thing. Though absent, the "thing," "concept," or "ideal" represented thus engenders its own hierarchies, its own series of pretenders, of supplicants, of discourses that busily mask its absence.

Contingent on the formation of a foundational logic is the hierarchization of the absent referent—thing, concept, ideal—over its/their present representative: words. Discourses are then seen as multiple, and "things," "concepts," and "ideals" as singular, originary, transcendental, and the former always already dependent on the hegemony of the latter. Subsequently, a second order of signification is created, that between spoken and written words, the latter denigrated because of their further removal from the speaking origin that designates discourse as its sufficient replacement. These two discourses, spoken and written, authorized to represent their signified's absence, carry on their discourses as the surface terrain of language. This surface erects itself as an opaque barrier that mediates (for) the father. No giddiness or fear of separation need emerge, for the words spoken fill in, albeit temporarily, for the (absent) paternal origin. The textual authority is imagined as only temporarily "offstage" and is still able to control and structure the proceedings of discourse through his image by perpetually threatening to reappear and reestablish order. In such an economy, discourse is then controlled from afar by an all-knowing, all-seeing theological foundation that both gives credence to discourse and militates against any patricidal abuses from within the terrain of representation. Even this certainty, however, is suspect. Foreman's "joke" on the misidentifed "authorities," and the inclusion of his own text in a perpetually backward-bending circle, render suspect the truthfulness of the written word. As a result, a certain ontological hysteria accompanies the ending of the play, for it becomes impossible to catalog accurately Foreman's joke.

In a sense, it is unfair to give away the ending of the play before it has begun, but, in another sense, the end is irrelevant. In Foreman's metaphysics, the end is always already contained in the beginning of representation, in the Voice that knows and guides the production. The processes employed in *Pandering to the Masses* recreate onstage the duopoly of representation; through the Voice, Foreman mimics both the (absent) voice of the signified and the theological play of the signifiers within the space traditionally assigned to the signifier. Rather than allowing the closure of representation to spin anonymously and omnipotently, the taped voice constantly foregrounds the discontinuous processes that construct "reality":

> *Voice:* He inhabits that word. That means, to celebrate his return, finally, he thinks about his face as being her face. . . . And worships it, finally. And reads it, finally, like a wonderful book. (35)

By reconstituting a narrative between Max, Rhoda, Ben, and the other characters, a narrative already constituted by the omniscient Voice (Foreman's voice, played over the theater's public address system), the pleasure of the narrative, the unfolding of a story, is denied, and the audience must either follow the narrative with a critical remove or vainly seduce itself into that narrative on the premise that it does so with the disconcertingly partial and fragmentary recognition of the process and consequences of the suture apparatus. "If a speech could be purely present, unveiled, naked, offered up in person in its truth, without the detours of a signifier foreign to it, if at the limit an undeferred *logos* were possible, it would not seduce anyone" (Derrida 1978, 71).

With the structure of representation constituted within the prologue, the play begins after the Voice announces its arrival.

> *Voice:* Ladies and gentlemen, announcing the ending of the prologue and the beginning of the play proper. (Foreman 1977, 19)

Indeed, at this point, *Pandering to the Masses* is no different from any other play in participating in the structures of representation. Having the Voice (of authority) onstage during a prologue is only one more stage technology for presenting the father. Foreman, however, begins to perturb this system by allowing the Voice to shift to active diegetic participation in the play once it begins. In so doing, the play is thus unable to conceal its own construction and slip silently into the space of representation; for representation and its other, the authority it is supposed to both conceal and represent, is also present onstage undermining its own function. Yet, in perturbing presence, the voice reestablishes another form of textual authority on another terrain. By calling attention to itself, the Voice, which structures the text, is able to draw attention away from the fact that its ability to identify itself as a kind of presence, or authority, renders it radically unable to be the authority behind the text and, consequently, is probably referring to some other site or terrain for its authority.

> *Voice:* The play *Fear* continues, by demonstrating what it is that apparently frightens the invisible Ben, which means the doubly invisible Max, which means that what is frightening is invisible now to the mathematical power 3,4,5,6,7,8,9. (24)

This awareness is finally unimportant to the Voice, for it is able to masquerade as the origin in the full knowledge that its masquerade is inconsequential, since the Voice's presence in the text still structures that discourse.

What the Voice does not and cannot know is that its textual authority is predicated on a slippage that constitutes a pre-originary *différance*. "There is always a surprise in store for the anatomy or physiology of any criticism that might think it had mastered the game, surveyed all the threads at once . . . without risking . . . the addition of some new thread" (Derrida 1982a, 63). If a shift in the power dynamics of the text does take place in *Pandering to the Masses*, it is because the Voice (authority, the father) must now take an active role in propagating its own representations. Consequently, what also appears onstage with any system of representation is that system's double, the space between the signifier and the signified that conceals the technology of representation. This space haunts Foreman's characters. Unable to deny that it exists, at the same time they cannot acknowledge its existence. Since it is in essence unrepresentable and unnameable, either acknowledgment or denial would inexorably rend the seamless fabric of representation. Such an acknowledgment would force the stage characters to concentrate on their own doubles as much as the other characters; a problematic, fragmented awareness that is only compounded because what can be known is only the presence of that gap, not its nature. By the end of *Pandering to the Masses* the characters must do "the dance of icons" (Foreman 1977, 36), of prelinguistic signifiers, in order to escape the impossibility of continuing with their narratives, narratives that have been rent by the emergence of the third term.

The end of *Pandering to the Masses* thus appears as another ruse. While Foreman wants to draw attention to the production of meaning at the level of the text, such a maneuver once again draws attention away from the technology of representation onto one of its constituents, short-circuiting the eruption of that discourse. Though Rhoda and her cohorts' flight to a terrain of icons represents an escape, the narrative function of the Voice arrests that flight, bringing it back into the problematic of representation. Indeed, there is an overwhelming sense that the Voice will not let go, cannot risk losing control, lest the hysteria behind representation reemerge, shattering the play's tightly constructed control network.

Foreman's later plays further explore the impossibility of a complete awareness of theater's double. *Film Is Evil, Radio Is Good* signals a return (or maybe a retreat) to traditional notions of textuality. *Film Is Evil*, unlike *Pandering to the Masses* or his other works, is one of Foreman's few texts that, without too much difficulty, could be produced and directed by somebody besides the author. Indeed, among the conventionalizing devices of *Film Is Evil* are the inklings of at least three distinct psychologically based characters, a conventional plot (however problematically formed), and the beginnings of certain diegetic technologies that enforce a suspension of disbelief. A further surprise is Foreman's own absence onstage except in the film sequence in which his face stares out at the audience, a blind observer who apparently no longer participates in his own authorial ruse of presence. By allowing his characters ostensibly to speak for themselves, he conceals the textual authority that he formerly sought to expose under a guise of agency.

In *Film Is Evil*, Foreman no longer relies on his own presence to foreground or suture the gap but, instead, investigates textual mechanisms through which to contain the eruption of the signifier-signified duopoly within the play's diegetic space. Unlike the end of *Pandering to the Masses*, in which the characters needed to call upon icons in order to escape the crushing embrace of the closure of representation, in *Film Is Evil*, the characters remain unified. The boundaries of discourse are still present onstage, however; at the end of the play, various figures appear with placards reading Charity, Virtue, and Truth, as does a snowman. Unspeaking and unnoticed (except for the snowman) in the diegetic space, Charity, Virtue, and Truth are active as tropes that ironically present the same philosophical boundaries as did the three texts at the end of *Pandering to the Masses*. The placard/tropes are, in a sense, the limits of an already very limited discourse, for such boundaries, consciously created onstage, can draw attention to those boundaries and thus perhaps prevent the discursive suturing that takes place between stage and life in the realistic drama. The snowman, however, assures that simple connections between the stage and life will not be made. When he appears with the three tropes, their solemn function as discursive governors is summarily derailed, and they break down into parodies of their tropic identities. Like the misidentified authors in *Pandering to the Masses*, the snowman disrupts the creation of discursive boundaries within the traditional space of representation onstage.

While participating in the diegetic space of the narrative, Estelle Merriweather, the central character in *Film Is Evil*, is almost a parody of herself:

> *Kate:* I think you're disappearing with somebody else's private property! Helen? Come back with that shell or I'll be very upset, and I'll zoom, zoom to a big, bad conclusion. After all, nobody goes public—even radiowise—without a protective layer or two—which I perfected over many years. Perhaps because I'm a fractionally frustrated woman who works in a radio station that slips and slides over the dial as if it were a banana peel, I've come face-to-face with the facts of life in general—man has failed. (154)[6]

Confined within a well-defined cultural stereotype of woman, her actions draw attention to themselves merely through her function as the receptacle of inculturated expectations. For the devices of the diegetic narrative to take place, her discourse must therefore be a discourse of limits. Because of the idiosyncrasies of this character, the text does not allow an unproblematic psychological identification with the character but, instead, invites its reader to identify with Merriweather at the same time he or she is given the lie about Merriweather's discourse.

At the same time as Estelle Merriweather and her tropes are presenting the mechanisms and audience effects of identification, one cannot help but suspect Foreman's attempt to perturb the space of representation from the inside. *Film Is Evil* completes the closure of representation by giving its characters a conclusive finitude at the end.

> *Richard:* That's why . . . the medium of the radio . . . is so superior
> to the medium of film. . . . Quiet. Quiet. And then We can hear
> what they are. Really. (Foreman 1987, 176)

Without some disruptive endgame, one must wonder if merely mocking certain limits and boundaries will dispel the hegemony of a sutured narrative. The play ends with "Richard's" voice on tape, singing:

> *Richard:* Radio Rick is on the air. . . . Radio Rick transmits a smile.
> While Richard sits and waits a while. (176)

Even though "Richard" appears to humor narrative closure, the play reconnects to itself by absorbing "Richard" into the diegesis and thereby allowing the drama to continue spinning toward closure.

Without the authorial voice onstage to provide guidance, the characters are forced to establish their own order, to fill in the void left by the vacationing father so that their drama can continue. If there is no drama on the theological stage without the father masquerading as present, in one form or another, then Foreman's exit cannot be seen as an escape from that presence but, rather, must be considered a reestablishment of another, more traditional order of representation. For a theater like Foreman's, the consequences of this reestablished absence are vast. Is the shift from the presence of *A* father, an individual, and accountable within the space of representation (another ruse further disguising the absence of the father), to the reinsertion of the nonpresence of *THE* father, the authority behind the text, indicative of a shift in Foreman's interest in problematizing the discourse of representation? In this play, his characters are responsible for maintaining parental narratives—for being "good sons." This change from staging the technologies of representation to exploring the labyrinth of ego-psychology-based characterization, however, does not simply equate with an unwillingness to examine representation, and it would be shortsighted to think that Foreman has gone the way of American realism. Rather than assimilating a realistic aesthetic, something that is preposterous even to think in Foreman's theater, the structures of representation, so mercilessly expounded in his earlier work, have found a more subterranean topology on which to work themselves out.

The control Foreman maintains over his dramas finally is disturbing, given his project of wanting to "make ourselves see." Even as Foreman shows the way to watch the theater falling precisely apart, one cannot be sure that he is not simply opening theatrical technologies without following through on the consequences of their actions. Perhaps it is in the intensely exact patterns in which he wants the theater to fall, perhaps it is in the none too subtle way he offers his own view as a replacement for the teleologies he wishes to complicate. In either case, Foreman's own process, especially his strong directorial voice, leaves open to suspicions of the worst kind his claim for making "us see ourselves seeing." In this light, two objections arise in regard to Foreman's work and, for that matter, the ontological project it embraces.

The first is that, in his analysis of the technology of representation, his gender bias is obvious. "Foreman has created a theatre from and for his likeness, which is itself a meaningful act. A feminist

spectator is obviously unforeseen in his work . . . a feminist fil-
ter . . . belies Foreman's claims" (Dolan 58). In her book *The Feminist
Spectator as Critic,* Jill Dolan confronts Foreman's performance aesthetic as solipsistically male oriented, an attribute that, as she de-
tails, excludes a feminist perspective: "Foreman constructs images of
women as enticing products that he assumes male spectators will
very much want to consume, either visually or through monetary
exchange" (52). If, in *Film Is Evil,* Merriweather is used as a trope, a
definable level of discourse, then it seems, following Dolan's critique, that Foreman is using woman as an idealized figure on which
to focus his narrative. Constituting woman as a boundary within
which masculist discourse can theatricalize its teleological drama effectively reduces her to an object, silenced and forgotten. Foreman's
practice represents women in much the same way Laura Mulvey and
other film theorists have argued that the classic Hollywood cinema
represents the (female) body. In addition, the use of women as
tropes also demands that they be thus considered as representing an
essential "womanhood," a cultural practice that, in its ahistoricism,
elides the material reality of life *sous râture.* The implications of these
two objections both point out some of the shortcomings in the philosophical model Foreman uses and betray the particular social specificity of such an artist.

Dolan's critique of Foreman's Ontological Hysteric Theatre focuses
on its specular dimensions, on the visual diegesis. In many of Foreman's plays, including *Pandering to the Masses,* nude women appear
onstage, so many so that it seems almost a signature gesture, at least
in the production photographs that accompany books and articles
on Foreman. According to Dolan, the nude woman's appearance
focuses the male spectator's gaze, incarcerating that woman into a
subject/object relationship with the spectator. This relationship thus
replicates society's treatment of women as inconsequential objects for
male pleasure, for, even while Foreman ostensibly problematizes that
economy by shining bright lights at his gazing audience, interrupting
their pleasure, he still constructs women as commodities, whether
obtainable or not.

Yet the simple suggestion that, in presenting nude women on-stage, Foreman undercuts his entire ontological project is in a sense a partial reading. The context in which Foreman presents his images, the frequent use of loud noises and bright lights to disrupt the spectatorial pleasure, must also be considered. It seems at least open to debate whether "pleasure" actually obtains in the context of the apparatus of psychological torture that Foreman constructs on-stage; the bright lights and disruptive noise are certainly reminiscent of the early Living Theatre's confrontational politics and, as such, seem to ironize any conventional "pleasure" that appears. Furthermore, Dolan is unwilling to acknowledge the nude men onstage except as elements that further foreground the visual pleasure of the male spectator. Certainly, Dolan's point that "the male body does not signify the history of exchange set up for male visual pleasure, the nude male is not the object of the exchange. A male body cannot be objectified in the same way a woman's can" (55) would suggest that Foreman is not simply replacing the sign of "woman" with that of "man." While Dolan maintains that nude men can only serve to accentuate woman's "lack," from a different perspective, the staging of a male body in a commodity position could be seen as a strategy for disrupting the simple equation of woman with commodity. Certainly, Foreman's staging of nude women is problematic. But it could be argued that Foreman attempts to call into question his own position as *auteur* by using the images of nude women as an aspect of ideological autocritique. In a theater in which the implications of traditional representation are so mercilessly examined, in which every element is deliberately charged to provoke the audience into a confrontation with the spectatorial consciousness to "see oneself seeing," Foreman confronts the impossibility of seeing outside his own condition within a representational structure that relies on voyeurism.

Yet Foreman trips himself up at this point as per Dolan's critique, for he appears to forget his own advice to "see oneself seeing," to be self-reflective, once he puts naked women onstage. "The aim is to discover how to live with lucidity and detachment amidst the powerful allure of this naked body. The ideal is not to be ruffled by it, but to create stage excitement that neutralizes its powerful tendency to pull focus" (qtd. in Dolan, 50). Foreman's blind spot to his own complicity in perpetuating standard representations of women indeed undermines his claims for an apperceptive stage experience, pace Dolan. Once Foreman decides that he can survey all the threads of his "game," and control its construction, it becomes apparent that he is in for a surprise.

Foreman's assumption that he can control the perception of objects onstage regardless of their ideological status or function, without adding more to that perception than he himself can account for, is predicated on his belief in his ability to determine fully the meaning of his words and images. This belief presents the same problem, however, that semiotics and structuralism have with language, for the word itself is only problematically programmable (Derrida 1978). By reading Foreman's phenomenological approach through Derrida, Dolan's critique can be extended. At some point in the generation of sign systems, of languages, the always already absent referent must be reckoned with. Discourse must at some point acknowledge the fact that one of its functions is to elide an absence. That the need for such representation is motivated in the first instance by a need to organize and identify an undefinable territory inhabited by lack and violence threatens the notion that language merely fills in a temporary absence. Furthermore, such a space is symptomatic of the play of desire within representation, a play that motivates the impulse toward language. Ultimately, the recognition of the absence behind the word is also the realization that presence can never be attained through representation. What is revealed in and by the space of representation is in fact a nonspace, a radically unfillable gap between the word and the thing. The turn away from presence to representation, to the word, signals the crossing into a space of no return, for, once within representation, language will never allow the return to presence; will never allow, for it is never possible, a "cathexing" proximity. "The present . . . is not primal but, rather, reconstituted . . . it is not the absolute, wholly living form which constitutes experience . . . there is no purity of the living present" (Derrida 1978, 212).

The existence of a text precludes the possibility of presence. There is no presence, furthermore, no metaphysical whole, truth, or being, behind the word, only the apparatus and structures of a "writing machine," or language, that may *represent* the psyche in the form of a text but never extends beyond representation. "But we must be wary of this formulation: there is no life present *at first* which would *then* come to protect, postpone, or reserve itself in *différance*" (Derrida 1978, 203). In other words, there is no self, no presence, before the fact of representation. The unchartable space between the object and its representation functions as a smoke screen, hiding the lost referent and thus enabling representation to prolong its illusion of ontological security for the self. Without that distance, in the phenomenological experience of absolute proximity, the self would lose its bearings and unifications and cease to exist. Consequently, when faced with the unnameable, the self plunges into an hysterical attempt to shore up its resources, to protect its illusions of continuity that an ontological presence would destroy. The self remains in a state of hysteria as it constantly assigns meanings to representations and as it formulates transcendental operatives designed to protect it from an awareness of its own precarious position within language. "Differences in the production of the trace may be reinterpreted as moments of deferring . . . this movement is described as the effort of life to protect itself by *deferring* a dangerous cathexis, that is, by constituting a reserve" (202).

It is here, in the initial doubling of identity that serves as an escape from the unnameable life force, and the consequent appearance of desire, that the scene of representation cultivates its terrains and territories. Once the self has identified itself, securing its position against the unnameable, it can continue the identity/desire process, distinguishing other objects, other areas, and assigning them linguistic territories, representing them to itself as external constructions over which the self gains control. This process effectively contains the doubling that instigates the theology of representation, the displacement of being, and the formation of a representational surface. By providing an occluding technology that constructs the illusion of an absolute proximity to presence (for language/representation keeps presence at bay), by preventing an awareness of the space between the signified and the signifier (that "gap" wherein the technologies of representation play out their dramas), representation suppresses both ontological violence and hysteria.

For representation to appear seamless and contingent solely on its transcendental affiliations, the technology operative in the gap, the third term that motivates the semiotic binary, must constitute a foundation upon which representation can safely exist as well as mask its operations. (In this space-between, the theological stage maintains and perpetuates its control.) Yet, if the transparency of these operations begins to fracture, or if the space between the signifier and signified erupts, foregrounding its presence, then the seamless code of representation (signifier/signified, Saussure's binomial sheet of paper) can no longer maintain itself. Indeed, the technology of the theological stage works only if its strictures of closure and unity are closely adhered to, if the authority of the signified is not questioned and the authenticity of the signifier not doubted. While the smugness of representation may be directly related to the influence of its particular *episteme*, by performing the theatricality of the gap, of the technologies of representation, the theological stage could perhaps "fall to pieces precisely" as Foreman hopes in his manifestos.

By remaining within the phenomenologically marked "theater" of representation, Foreman's autocritique stops at the point of its own unrepresentibility, where the stage might fall apart according to a logic other than Foreman's. While it seems questionable that Foreman explicitly "subscribes to a conservative ideology," given his intense efforts to deconstruct the stage and his problematization of the ontological status of the object on/of that stage, that he does so without a clear sense of the ideological investments of his objects appears to limit the critique that finally emerges. Foreman's two plays evince a blindness to the repetition of the author-creator mechanisms that Derrida defines as the signature gesture of the theological stage. While they investigate the authorial mechanisms of textuality, they fail to account for the assumptions that underlie their own discourse. Derrida's point that any criticism or reading that remains blind to its complicity in the production of meaning will constantly "lose the thread" of the text through imagining that it can stand back and surmise the text as a distinct unit returns to haunt Foreman. In being so seduced by its own power of criticism, Foreman's Ontological Hysteric Theatre remains compliant with the metaphysics within which the text-as-object itself, rather than as representation of deferred presence, belongs. In addition, this nonreflexive criticism assures its participation in the political configurations that embody the very metaphysical tradition that Foreman hopes to disrupt and, in fact, provide a sound argument for retaining a sense of the impossibility of "mastering all the threads."

In many regards, Fassbinder's theater is the antithesis of Foreman's, and indeed the rest of the Western theater tradition, for Fassbinder has no compunction about letting the stage fall to pieces willy-nilly. Unlike Foreman, he seeks no apparent recuperation of that space into a new form but, instead, wants to challenge and ultimately disrupt its entire apparatus. His characters are not alternative visions, deconstructing and reconstructing themselves onstage, but, rather, hypercharacters, simulations of characters who, in overcoding their particular designation, render bankrupt the traditional formation of character and narrative. Excessive simulation as a resistive and disruptive force is central to Fassbinder's work both in the theater and in the cinema.

Since the first round of realism, the dominant Eurocentric theater has sought to create a stage experience in which the characters appear as real as life. While there have been many challenges to this effort, most of these have based their dissent on an alternative "true" representation of a person, however differently constituted. Fassbinder works for a characterization that is not simply real but realer than real, indeed, hyperreal overcodifications of the traditional boundaries of character and of social mores that make the humanist principles upon which they are based functionally obsolete. Neither inside nor outside the frame of representation, these characters disrupt the mechanisms by which they are constituted.

Fassbinder's philosophical project connects to his political agenda. Whereas the aesthetics of capitalism and liberal humanism support a seemingly benign social order, Fassbinder's plays reveal a form of fascism lurking not far beneath this aesthetic surface. Fassbinder ties the emergence of this form of personal fascism both to the historical fascism that reached its initial apotheosis in the 1930s under national socialism and to the rise of State capitalism as a controlling force in Western Europe and the United States. The concrete manifestation of social and economic fascism in the Federal Republic of Germany is the subject of his last play, *Garbage, The City and Death*. In similar manner, but in more philosophical or metaphysical form, it is also the subject of his play *Blood on the Cat's Neck*.

In *Garbage, The City and Death*, the fascism that underlies capitalist relationships is confronted by an anarchy within the representations of the characters. Pushed to extremes, the characters embody a force that is disruptive of the metaphysics of character that structure the traditional stage. Rather than simply representing anarchists, or anti-Semites, they have passed up a "moral" existence based on identification (with the Same) to become "phantasms" that reveal the mechanisms of domination at work in the Platonic hierarchalization of copies and representation. Fassbinder leaves his ontological and epistemological project unexplored in this play, however. Instead, he defers the philosophical consequences of its "aesthetic existence" onto a political terrain. In the earlier play, *Blood on the Cat's Neck* (subtitled *Marilyn Monroe and the Vampires*), he explores the possibility of a textuality that in fact destroys the representational network of the stage.

In *Blood on a Cat's Neck*, Phoebe Zeitgeist "has been sent to the earth from a distant star to write an eyewitness account of human democracy. But Phoebe Zeitgeist, . . . although she has learned the words, doesn't understand human language" (Fassbinder 1985a, 97). Phoebe (moon goddess disguised as a virgin hunter) has a problem: she, the spirit of her times, does not understand the language and therefore cannot participate in the writing of her history. She is present in the play only as a border, a boundary around which the other characters play out their drama. In the first section, the other characters talk to her, at her, about their lives and situations in a series of monologues. Phoebe, because she does not know the language, can be only an unspeaking (unspeakable) presence. The others, ostensibly portraying humanist dramas of life, sex, death, and food, interact with each other, but not with Phoebe. They talk to her, but only as something mute and other. She is the frame, the uncrossable limit by which their discourse is measured.

In the second part, when Phoebe speaks, she does so only in aped fragments culled from the conversations around her. Her speech, a series of nonsequiturs, is further set off by the fact that she has no interaction with anyone else onstage. In addition, her words are printed in capitals on the page. By diacritically separating her, each enunciation marks the limit of the others' discourse and provides a physical barrier that signals the end and beginning of each of the other characters' various vignettes.

Is Phoebe set off from the economy of the earth people because she is an alien, or is her alienation indicative of a certain discursive position? She is inserted, inserts herself, into the discourse throughout the play as if to inspect or interrogate the other agents for the writing of her history. Yet, in the first half, she is silent and, in the second, present only as a mysteriously incoherent commentator. Consequently, she remains apart from the play's normative economies. Object for neither the Soldier's, Lover's, or Policeman's lust nor confidant for the Dead Soldier's Wife nor foil for the Mistress or Model, she remains outside of any inscriptive framework, not apart from, but as the limit to the drama. Yet she appears onstage and thus must be included in the play's desiring economies. The manner in which she does, however, problematizes the notion of a subject/object relationship.

Rather than simply conforming to either the subject or object model, Phoebe acts as a speculum, a tertiary insert into the textual duopoly. "Woman is neither open nor closed. She is indefinite, in-finite, *form is never complete in her*. She is not infinite but neither is she *a* unit(y)" (Irigaray 1985, 229). The incompleteness of woman, in Iri-garay's formulation, prevents (male) discourse from ascribing her to a specific function, except through imagining her as fundamentally defective. But if this prescriptive defect is rejected as a phallogocen-tric ruse, the discursive violence inherent in the "prescriptions of a hom(m)osexual imaginary" (229) can be reversed, not simply as retribution for textual misogyny but also to raise an irresolution: "For (the) woman neither is able to give herself some meaning by speech nor means to be able to speak in such a way that she is assigned to some concept or that some fixed notion is assigned to her" (230). By establishing a textual terrain without subjects and objects, the/a woman rearranges that space not as a teleological deferment but, rather, as a topology of jouissance that is unrecuperable by phallocratic discourse.

By not speculating on the other characters' discourse, Phoebe Zeitgeist inserts herself into the text's discourse as an observer, both as Irigaray's Other Woman and as an alien. By remaining outside the textual logic, she forms an uncrossable lacuna, framing and disrupting its authority. If a function of the theological stage is to recuperate divergent elements into economies that territorialize or reterritorialize both women and transgressive behavior in order to establish the transcendence of the father, and to suppress any false or bad claimants, then Phoebe acts as a boundary whose presence perturbs his discourse by her refusal to participate. Rather than remaining as the Other/object, a passive female on which unspeakable acts of violence are played out in the drama, she acts like the/a woman who cannot be inscribed. As such, she is unimaginable to the Platonic "hom(m)osexual" discourse, which cannot imagine her except as female/object. Phoebe, by remaining incoherent, shatters the structures necessary to maintain the other characters' narratives. Phoebe both speaks and does not speak; the indetermination that arises also reveals, in the same moment, that which is concealed by the closure of representation: the father's absence and the simulacrum that perforce takes his place. In the context of her inarticulate disruptions, her words without a language, so to speak, Phoebe presents herself not only as a bad copy who has lost her way but also the return of the force that Platonism sought to extinguish.

Phoebe Zeitgeist is not simply a transgressive agent. She never sutures into the economy of the earth characters, is never reorganized as woman (other than man), nor inscribed as a site of discursive pleasure. Instead, she marks the earth people with her discourse (literally, with her teeth), the discourse of the Other Woman, the elided voice, and thus compels them into simulation. She takes over their words and, in doing so, makes those words as alien as she is, makes it impossible for them to continue on with their personal narratives. When she appropriates their language, Phoebe operates as a pre-originary "becoming," as a simulacrum rather than a fixed location. Indeed, her presence perturbs the complacency that privileges the father and his logoi over a pre-originary *différance*, a simulacrum not dependent on the (absent) father for signification.

By the end of the play, the other characters are as unable as Phoebe to articulate a coherent grammar. As she mimics their confusion while biting them, they fall out of the organizing discourse into which they originally sought to inscribe Phoebe. Quite unexpectedly, though, and against the desiccating babble at the end of the world of discourse, she ends the play by quoting Kant:

A concept is not, however, determined in a purely abstract manner; understanding is to be differentiated from reason, therefore, in the comprehension of concepts as a whole. (125)

This strategic reentry into high German philosophy, ensconced as it is in the "destiny of the West," parodies the other characters' complete loss of their comprehensive facilities and disrupts her position as the silent woman.

In considering Phoebe, the inapplicability of the notion of a body that writes itself (and, in doing so, perturbs discourse) is immediately apparent, for Phoebe, in reverting to Kant, dispels the expectation that she will ground discourse in her Otherness. On the other hand, Irigaray's (re)theorization of the/a woman in the context of metaphysics is important to my own project, for it both represents a continuation of the critique of metaphysics underlying my argument and reveals a further aspect of Fassbinder's critique—his radical unfounding of difference. Indeed, while Fassbinder's sexual politics lead far afield from Irigaray—he has no intention of recuperating any form of sexuality as a liberative experience, unless that experience is a sadomasochistic pleasure—Irigaray theorizes the Other of Platonism in such a way that makes clear that only in the economy of the Same does such "Otherness" obtain a negative charge.

Phoebe Zeitgeist's seduction and subsequent abandonment of the other characters at the end of *Blood on the Cat's Neck* exemplifies how Fassbinder apparently begins to adopt Irigaray's notion of woman-as-speculum, as I have argued. But the manner in which Phoebe leaves those characters to their own demise is far from what Irigaray imagines. At the end of the play, when she has the characters babbling incoherently—that is, speaking in (her) tongues, saying words that have no grammatological connections—rather than rewarding them for participating in her (Other) language, she reverts to the father, Immanuel Kant. The density of the quote in relation to the vapid conversations of the other characters, the formality of the language, is enough to insure that it will be accessible only to those thoroughly familiar with the Western philosophical tradition; when Phoebe brings this conception of reason and understanding to the text, it subverts her previous counterdiscourse by betraying the assumption that she has been speaking non-sense, that she is Other and thus erased. The other participants are thus left babbling incoherently rather than participating in the discourse (Irigaray's Other Woman) promised in the shift from Plato/man to Phoebe/woman. The text constructs a countererotics, based on Phoebe's Otherness, to seduce the characters away from the erotics of the father. But, when Phoebe reverts to Kant, that discourse "goes weightless" (loses its primary referent) and reveals a universe as cruel and inhospitable as the one in which the characters of *Garbage, The City and Death* exist.

The sexual politic that emerges from both texts is mercilessly violent. These characters live in a delirious world that is, in a sense, beyond misogyny and anti-Semitism and into S&M scare tactics, a world, that is, that refuses to subsume the excess of desire to a unitary logic of one sort or another. Unable to find the pleasure that marks Irigaray's the/an Other Woman's *écriture*, they remain in an incontinent state that marks the end of Platonism. "The Other is [in Platonism], indeed, not only a defect that affects images; it, itself, appears as a possible model as against the good model of the Same"

(Deleuze 1990, 262n). Relentlessly unable to provide an alternative to the nihilism and brutality of a simulated universe, Fassbinder's characters revel in their own destruction and, in the process, reveal the consequences of a metaphysics based on an imaginary real.

Seen in the context of modes of production and utilitarianism, which serve a teleological necessity, *Blood on the Cat's Neck* is an alternative application of the logic of deconstruction, one that substitutes an empty bracket of anarchy (de[ ]struction) for the "con" game of metaphysics. Fassbinder attacks metaphysics, as he does politics, from the position of that framework's Other: "The simulacrum is built upon a disparity or upon a difference. It internalizes a dissimilarity. . . . If the simulacrum still has a model, it is another model, a model of the Other from which there flows an internalized dissemblance" (258). The appearance of the Other on the post-structured stage has consequences that extend well beyond the limit of any one text and, in fact, begin to constitute a notion of theatricality. In Fassbinder's text, the Other functions in a manner that is initially similar to that of Irigaray's Other Woman but that soon becomes the harbinger of a sadomasochistic erotics unimagined by Irigaray. In fact, the simulacrum takes on immediate political attributes in Fassbinder's later play, *Garbage, The City and Death*. At the end of *Blood on the Cat's Neck,* Phoebe Zeitgeist has reduced the other characters to babbling. She alone remains to speak, yet the value of what she says is ambiguous. In *Garbage, The City and Death*, the characters are simulacra as well, but the political implications of their actions are altogether too apparent.

Garbage, The City and Death was influenced by the immediate social and economic conditions in Frankfurt and, by analogy, in Western capitalism. Unlike his other more allegorical theater works, this play can only be understood in its immediate context: Frankfurt's housing crisis in 1965–67. Frankfurt in the 1970s was considered the Federal Republic of Germany's emblem of success and industry, of its ability to bounce back from the desolation of 1945. Indeed, the parallels between Frankfurt and cities in the United States (a comparison made in the play) is all the more ironic (for Fassbinder) since it was U.S.

money that allowed the Federal Republic to rebuild. At the time, an entire sector of low-cost housing was allowed to be rezoned for industrial use. Such speculation enriched the landowners and forced the poor and working-class residents to give up their homes, further exacerbating an already pronounced class division. *Garbage, The City and Death* was in part a reaction to these conditions, as the play explores the processes and effects of those who created and were disenfranchised by the housing crisis. In the late 1960s and early 1970s, Frankfurt's "Westend" district, home to German national and foreign workers, students, prostitutes, and a large transient population, was seen as prime industrial territory, ripe for development but for the dilapidated apartment buildings and undesirable population. The real estate concerns procured zoning ordinances to level the district. The Westend inhabitants, however, were not so acquiescent. Consequently, many rich landowners either forcibly evicted their tenants or, failing to do so, allowed the buildings to deteriorate until they were uninhabitable. In other cases, when tenants refused to leave, the police would come in to evict them forcibly, a strategy that almost guaranteed the ensuing riots. Consequently, the area became a symbol of what was wrong with the economic system of the modern Federal Republic.[7]

Fassbinder's critique of capitalism does not posit a simple alternative, a "good/bad" scenario composed of positive and negative characters. Instead, he suggests that the entire social structure of Frankfurt is complicit in creating the intolerable conditions his characters suffer. The play takes place in the leather bars and cafés of Frankfurt and focuses on four characters: Roma B, a prostitute; her pimp, Franz B.; Müller, the former Nazi; and The Rich Jew. These four characters are surrounded by a host of prostitutes, leather men, lackeys, and undercover policemen with vaguely literary names, including Fräulein Emma von Waldenstein, Asbach-Lilly, Marie-Antoinette, The Little Prince, and Hellfritz, Tenor. Roma B. is slowly dying of tuberculosis because Franz forces her to work outdoors on bitterly cold nights to pay for his gambling debts and beats her when she fails.

Franz B.: Now?

Roma B.: Don't hit.

Franz B.: Who hits you? The one who loves you hits you. So? Who hits you?

Roma B.: You—love me, so. . .

Franz B.: So I hit you if I love you. But I can't love you all day long and all night long. And then all day long again. How much?. . . So? How much?! I get it. Nothing again. That's the third time this week.

Roma B.: It was cold, Franz. My legs were turning to stone. I did gymnastics, deep breathing. Finally even prayed. It was hours. No one came. Like a jinx.

Franz B.: And now? How do I look? Can I let myself be seen with the rest of them, the successful ones? Can I drink a beer in good conscience: won't the others notice me, failure pasted on my brow?

Roma B.: I beg your forgiveness.

Franz B.: What's your forgiveness to me? To die in humility like this is miserable. Give me freedom, Roma, and freedom is money. It's Saturday, the Bank's closed. The racetrack awaits. I must do what I must do. Go. Work. Quickly and successfully. And produce! (1985b, 166)

Roma B. is forced out into the cold to produce where she meets The Rich Jew.

Roma B.: *(Coughing hard.)* Happiness is not always fun.

The Rich Jew: Last testament from the emphysema ward.

Little Prince: That's Roma B., boss, she's constantly freezing.

The Rich Jew: Cities are cold and it's only fitting that people freeze there. Why do they build themselves such cities?

Dwarf: *(Suffers a fit of laughing.)* (168)

Gradually, The Rich Jew realizes who Roma B. is and how she would be useful to him, so he takes her away from Franz B. Franz B. then discovers his own homosexuality, reversing his position of dominance over Roma B. to one of being dominated. Meanwhile, The Rich Jew takes Roma B. as a mistress because her father, Müller, was a technocrat in a concentration camp, responsible for murdering The Rich Jew's parents.

> *Müller:* I wasn't concerned with each and every one of the people I murdered. I wasn't an individualist. I am a technocrat. But it's possible I am his parents' murderer, I'd be glad of it. And I am glad of it. (185)

Müller ducks out on his responsibility for the Holocaust by becoming a transvestite and sharing clothing and makeup with his wife. By keeping Roma B., The Rich Jew exacts revenge on Müller. Roma B., who is on a quest for love, despairs of her life when she realizes why The Rich Jew loves her, and she begs him to kill her, which he does.

> *The Rich Jew:* I noticed you need me.
> *Roma B.:* I failed.
> *The Rich Jew:* Don't talk.
> *Roma B.:* I renounce my role. It doesn't satisfy me.
> *The Rich Jew:* The show's over. Anyway you have already fulfilled your purpose.
> *Roma B.:* I've known that for some time. I forgave you.
> *The Rich Jew:* You have no right to forgive me. It's none of your concern.
> *Roma B.:* I know what's due me. I have no right to forgive, no right to demand. No rights at all. That's my only hope. Abject. Powerless. That's my only hope. . . .
> *The Rich Jew:* I could forgive you if I wanted to.
> *Roma B.:* Yes but I don't accept your forgiveness. You're no comfort to me.
> *The Rich Jew:* Are you so sure?
> *Roma B.:* No. Maybe you are right. Maybe once more it is you who I need.

The Rich Jew: You have already thought things through.
Roma B.: Yes. I want to die. (187)

After The Rich Jew strangles Roma B. with his necktie, the scene shifts to the chief of police's office (who turns out to be Müller's son). The Rich Jew's assistants are killed in order to remove witnesses to the murder, and Franz B. is brought in, having been fisted into un-consciousness. Finally, Müller II and The Rich Jew conspire to frame him as Roma B.'s murderer.

Garbage, The City and Death depicts a more or less real-time situation, the condition of the city in the Federal Republic. The play can be read as an allegory for the modern condition under late capitalism, a set of circumstances that suffers no human comfort and that tolerates no illusions about the dominant structures of everyday life.[8] It is also an addition to a series of German plays about fascism that signify a level of understanding that goes beyond simple moralistic responses, such as Peter Weiss's *The Investigation* and Rolf Hochhuth's *The Deputy*. The position of *Garbage, The City and Death* vis-à-vis the older drama is apparent when reading Andreas Huyssen's review of an earlier generation's attempt at writing plays about fascism and the Holocaust in Germany, about the process of *Vergegenheits-bewältigung* (or coming to terms with the past). For Huyssen, "the key problem . . . is not so much the presence or absence of historically recognizable events or characters but rather the question of identification" (105). Huyssen suggests that the failure of coming to terms with the past in the earlier drama is due to an avoidance of actual identification with the agents involved in the Holocaust for a reconstruction of historically accurate dramatizations. Fassbinder inverts this process by creating allegorical characters and events that are readily identifiable as fascistic. Rather than pursuing diegetic recognition, Fassbinder seeks a form of abstraction that necessarily implicates the individual's participation in fascism and other social features of State capitalism.

The play's characters function as tropes that distinguish certain discursive boundaries within a terrain constructed from cultural "signposts." *Garbage, The City and Death* exploits the possibility of ambiguity within a terrain in which that notion, once a central tenet of humanist discourse, is presumably bankrupt, since here it is directly linked to fascism. Various scenes are framed by a *pas de deux*—either a song from the traditional "high culture" or popular culture; a duet from *La Traviata, Eine Kleine Nacht Musik,* a children's rhyme, or cabaret piece. For example, when Franz B. forces Roma B. to go back out into the cold to earn money, the scene ends with Asbach-Lilly and Hellfritz, Tenor, dancing to "Liebestod" from *Tristan und Isolde.* This device sets into relief the process by which traditional culture is contextualized, foregrounding the constructedness and contingency of what constitutes aesthetic pleasure. Indeed, the play pushes aside any naturalist basis for character and in its place asserts a politics of simulation.

> *Jim: (Sings.)* I'm just a journeyman traveler, good night, dear lady, good night. Quite thin is my jerkin, quite thick is my fur, good night, dear lady, good night.
> *Dwarf:* Spiders! Lots of little black spiders. The city is groaning under the spiders. It's trembling and moaning. The spiders are becoming a plague. They will be a plague until the city has learned to derive pleasure from them. Spiders! (180)

Coming at the end of the scene in which Roma B. leaves Franz B. for the last time, this coda pushes what has just happened into a realm that can hardly be considered real; however, neither can it be considered merely fantastical. Its content in relation to the scene is realer than real, or hyperreal, in that it creates a realm that contains vestiges of a real world but contains no direct relationship to one. The realm of the hyperreal, furthermore, provides a link between the political and philosophical projects in Fassbinder's plays, a link that Jean Baudrillard has defined as the "third order of simulation."

Baudrillard attacks Western aesthetics' privileging of a hierarchical relationship between the object and its representation and the moral ontology attendant on that relationship. His critique of representation starts with the collapse of hierarchies in late capitalism: "The very definition of the real becomes: *that of which it is possible to give an equivalent reproduction.* . . . At the limit of this process of reproducibil-ity, the real is not only what can be reproduced, *but that which is always already reproduced.* The hyperreal, . . . which is entirely in simu-lation" (1983c, 146). Systems of signification are structured by three possible logics that he defines in *Simulations:* the logic of the real, the logic of the reproducible, and the logic of the simulacrum, or the hyperreal. The first and second are systems that, in their transcen-dental teleologies, constitute a (Western) metaphysics. The third, however, marks a significant departure from teleology. The simula-crum is not merely a copy of the real, but a copy of a copy, a false copy designated by a model rather than by a resemblance to a "real" origin: "And so art is everywhere, since artifice is at the very heart of reality. And so art is dead, not only because its critical transcen-dence is gone, but because reality itself, entirely impregnated by an aesthetic which is inseparable from its own structure, has been con-fused with its own image" (151–52). Rather than representing an actual object, the sign circulates through channels of communication and exchange (controlled for the most part by large multinational corporations that dictate its composition according to the needs of their marketing strategies and that can also eliminate competition by their sheer size).

In the theater, the actor onstage is not the character that he or she portrays. What is missing from that very basic observation is the pretense, or suspension of disbelief, necessary for the theatrical econ-omy to proceed; in Baudrillard's scheme, this suspension is no longer possible, or viable, because, in the imploded social sphere of the third order of simulacra, illusionism cannot maintain its mechanisms. Baudrillard relates this argument to the impossibility of any theatrical representation of consequence: "End of the theatre of representation, the space of signs, their conflicts, their silence. . . . 'Its a theatre,' 'Its a movie,' old adages, old naturalistic denunciation. These sayings are now obsolete" (1982, 104). Theater might still take place, but its illu-sions can operate only as self-parody, or referentless thrill seeking in which the only measure of success is in the emulation of absolute circulation and exchange: metastatic speed. Furthermore, the ob-server too is bereft of perspective and so is sucked into "the whole chaotic constellation of the social" along with the observed (Baudrillard 1983b, 94). The end of the suspension of disbelief, the dissolution of drama into immediacy and visibility, also signals the disruption of the scene by the "obscene," of the intrigue of narrative with the fascination of the image. "Obscenity begins precisely when there is no more spectacle, no more scene, when all becomes transparence and immediate visibility, when everything is exposed to the harsh and inexorable light of information and communication (Baudrillard 1983a, 130). No longer alienated by production, since production has been replaced by circulation in the move from high to late capitalism, the "masses," the "workers," and the "individual"—i.e., any potentially oppositional group—fall into the seductive circulation of information and, consequently, are afforded no room or opportunity for resistance.[9] The bleakness, and seductiveness, of Baudrillard's giddy appraisal of a world marked by the cool digitality of the binary code is in a sense unavoidable when entering the realm of the simulacrum. Yet his "ob/scene" contains only one possibility for a politics of simulation.

As a result of the dismantling of Platonism that simulation enforces, Platonic moral categories—the foundation for hierarchalized discourse—also collapse, with a particularly disturbing result. In *The Logic of Sense*, Gilles Deleuze delineates this result as a significant threat to the order of the real, or the Same, and its representations: "As a consequence of searching in the direction of the simulacrum and of leaning over its abyss, Plato discovers, in the flash of an instant, that the simulacrum is not simply a false copy, but that it places in question the very notations of copy and model" (1990, 256). The distinction necessary to Platonism, the ability to separate the simulacrum from the real by constructing it as a false copy, as one of the images on the wall of the cave, becomes impossible because the simulacrum gains its own existence through invoking a world outside the mindless repetition of the Same that Platonism demands. For Deleuze, the simulacrum embodies its own creative potentials and disruptive forces. Built upon a dissimilarity rather than a model, the simulacrum implies "huge dimensions, depths and distances that the observer cannot master" (258) and thus is unaccountable to the Same or the Similar. By tying the simulacrum to Nietzsche's eternal return (a force that, through the generation of a serial logic, embodies a creative potential at each occurrence in its matrix) as something a priori outside of the Same and its representations, Deleuze finds in the simulacrum something other than does Baudrillard; rather than the pessimism of an obscene late capitalism, a "creative chaos" emerges that contributes to the disarray in which Platonism finds itself when confronted with its Other. The simulacrum is outside of that which can be contained in a system of icons and copies, a logic constituted in the power of the false, the phantasm that leaves no ground for the real.[10]

The legacy of the rise of the simulacrum invalidates systems of the real, because, as Baudrillard, Deleuze, and even Plato—finding "behind each cave another that opens still more deeply, and beyond each surface a subterranean world yet more vast, more strange" (Nietzsche 289)—could not in the end ignore, the simulacrum precedes and constitutes the real. This phantasm evokes chaos and, in doing so, sets in motion the disruption of the happily ordered world of representation; this chaos, furthermore, reveals the ineluctability of signs: "The secret of the eternal return is that it does not express an order opposed to the chaos engulfing it. On the contrary, it is nothing other than chaos itself, or the power of affirming chaos" (Deleuze 1990, 264). This creative chaos constitutes the difference between incarceration and liberation. The simulacrum, then, the "phantasm of theatre," pushes the stakes of verisimilitude to their absolute limit: "At bottom, the profound tactic of simulation . . . is to make the system collapse under an excess of reality" (Baudrillard 1983c, 120). What emerges is radical contingency, a notion absolutely counterposed to (though also often substituted for) transcendence. If moral categories, including those on which "the real" (hereafter bankrupt) are operative, they are so only as political categories: "The simulacrum is an image without resemblance. . . . We have become simulacra. We have forsaken moral existence in order to enter into aesthetic existence" (Deleuze 1990, 257). The substitution of politics for metaphysics in the realm of the simulacrum enables Deleuze to pursue the end of Platonism as a system that is based on the repression of its/the Other.

Morality and teleology become political under the sway of the hyperreal. With no definite basis such as a "god," there are no categorical imperatives outside the mode of exchange. In the imploded sponge of the social—the sphere to which Baudrillard relegates late capitalist society—it is not that there are no more consequences nor that agency becomes a useless, passive parody of itself but, rather, that any such notions now must carry the weight of their endemic implications, must be responsible for and to the world they have created. "Terrorists, killers, hostages, leaders, spectators, public opinion—*there is no more innocence in a system which has no meaning*" (Baudrillard 1983b, 116, italics added). For Baudrillard, terrorism becomes the only theater of any consequence, becomes "our Theatre of Cruelty," for it does not distinguish its victims on the basis of morality but, instead, in terms of culpability within systems of domination.[11]

Garbage, The City and Death pursues just such a conclusion. The characters—Roma B., Franz B., The Rich Jew—may be victims/Others of the system to more or less of a degree (the prostitute Roma and The Rich Jew seem the two extremes: one a victim of patriarchy and the other of history), but none remain unimplicated by the system that eventually incarcerates them. A subsequent problem in such a statement is that it could be used to assume that there is a degree of culpability in their implication, that, through some personal *mauvaise foi*, each of these characters has destined him- or herself to an individual hell. In part, however, the structure of *Garbage, The City and Death* prevents this from becoming a play about solipsism. With each sequence framed by a particular cultural artifact—a duet from *La Traviata*, for example—the play is pulled into a historical specificity that exists well outside its own diegesis. Each segment can be read as reflective of both the fascism within the play and that within the culture as a whole. The patterns of domination in *La Traviata* are replicated onstage between The Rich Jew and Roma B.; while the opera may be only a cultural artifact, the scene is a reminder that such things are replicated throughout society and need not be specific to any particular play.

The conflation of capitalism and fascism structures the play's erotic relationships, constituting a domain in which erotica *is* "fascistiod" (Fassbinder's term) domination:

> *Jim:* The hen that lays the golden egg, according to my father, is capital. Where am I going to find capital I wonder. Houses, properties. That's it I think, and I go for it. And the result? I barely make it. And Saturdays I treat myself: Two broads! (168)

The worlds of prostitution and of real estate speculation are paralleled, not to condemn either but, rather, to implicate the middle-class veneer that would place value judgments on both. In *Garbage, The City and Death*, erotics and money are inseparable:

> *The Rich Jew:* That's how it should be, and it's fitting. And peace and quiet, Madame, is amazingly gratifying. You don't have to respond.... This image is enchantingly beautiful, the city which devotes itself to ruin. So—come. Your diseased lungs should pay off for you. (169)

Whether it be the terrain of the prostitute—

> *Franz B.:* Now go. Do well and don't leave him in the lurch, the one who is there for you as you need him. Go little one, go and let yourself be fucked.... And be righteous. Men too are only human. (167)

—or that of the real estate speculator—

> *The Rich Jew:* The city needs the unscrupulous businessman who allows it to transform itself. It must protect him thank you very much. (171)

—both are seen as necessary configurations of the city, and the two go hand in hand:

> *The Rich Jew:* Cities are cold and it's only fitting that people freeze there. Why do they build themselves such cities? (168)

The fascistic undercurrents of capitalism arise in the complete subservience and the disintegration of autonomy or agency demanded by capitalist relationships, a confluence that reveals exchange as domination.

The fascism that structures these characters' lives does not appear in a moralistic fashion. Instead, the realities of these people's lives, the intense brutality and cold eroticism, are a direct consequence of their simulated world. Indeed, simulation as a scheme seems to be endowed with both negative and positive potentials.

> *Roma B.:* Despair—call it by its proper name, that'll raise you capital. (167)

As simulacra, agents without an imperative morality, their world is destructive and brutal, with love coming only through domination.

> *Roma B.:* I know you're right. You're right and kind, and you hit me as little as possible, and forgive me my sins. (166)

In fact, the whole notion of relationship is radically altered into a form of hyperconformity, a hyperdomination that is too good to be true.

> *Franz B.:* I love you! Shove your fists up my ass, tear me apart, let me hear the angels singing. . . . Do me good. Destroy me! (183)

If empathy need be based on an ulterior motive, a categorical notion of "good" or "humanity," something besides greed or domination, then these characters make a mockery of it. Their world is relentlessly harsh. The breakdown of those traditional categories in the face of late capitalism is not hidden under a veneer of humanism nor replaced by characters who comport some "good" sensibility.

> *Dwarf:* Oh my God, I thank you. He has killed her, he has disqualified himself. It's clear he loved her. Whoever loves has blown his rights. (188)

Each character and each relationship is exploited for its fascistic characteristics; every interaction dissolves beneath the weight of a capitalist universe.

> *Müller:* Yeah, and she lived longer than one could have expected.
> *Kraus, Peter:* So it goes. The city gobbles up its children. (188)

Müller, the ex-Nazi, is proud of his history; furthermore, within the ambiguity of a transvestite, he can consciously exploit his surface to achieve an artificial respectability. Hiding as a woman, he ruptures the politics of identification that would pin him down to any position.

> *Müller:* It's no burden to be a Jew killer when you have convictions like mine.
> *Roma B.:* And the degradation doesn't affect you?
> *Müller:* It's not really meant for me, but it does set you to thinking what kind of country this is which permits the kinds of things which occur here everyday. (185)

That he takes on the disguise of the oppressed while proudly reveling in his past deeds suggests the denial of fascism that Germany itself went through after World War II. By overcoding the pride of Müller, the ex-Nazi, Fassbinder foregrounds the banal integration of fascism into contemporary society.

Garbage, The City and Death is ostensibly a critique of real estate speculation and the gentrification of German cities as a part of the postwar economic restoration. Its stormy reception in Frankfurt, however, centered around its portrayal of certain social attitudes. The focal point of the controversy was the play's main character, "The Rich Jew." Read by the Jewish community and the political Right as an overtly anti-Semitic portrayal, this character invoked accusations of "left-wing fascism" from the German conservatives and of singling out the Jews as the cause of Frankfurt's social problems in the 1970s.[12] The reaction to this play is indicative of how the Federal Republic dealt with its National Socialist past and responsibility for the Holocaust: through (at least initially) sublimating and consequently denying any anti-Semitism and its attendant guilt.

In attacking the instigators of the dismal social conditions, *Garbage, The City and Death* burned the hands of two important groups. The Jewish population saw *Garbage, The City and Death* as an overt manifestation of the anti-Semitism in the Federal Republic at the time and objected on that basis. The Jewish community's reaction to *Garbage, The City and Death* certainly seems justifiable given its historical situation in Germany. What is surprising about its reaction—especially to the attempt to stage the play in 1985—is that it marked the first time since the Holocaust that the community protested openly against a perceived abuse.[13] The Rich Jew was seen as a continuation of the National Socialist attempt to blame Germany's economic problems on the Jewish community. That the character is not even given a proper name is seen as a confirmation of this view, as is his link to corrupt business practices. Similarly, the several overtly fascistic speeches in the play (especially those of the character Müller) were seen as Fassbinder's own. The piece was labeled an example of "political pornography" by E. L. Ehrlich of the B'nai B'rith in 1974 and remained unstaged for the next ten years.[14]

The Jewish indignation over Fassbinder's play is best understood in light of the Holocaust and the "final solution." Jews experienced National Socialism as an attempt to silence an entire race. As such, the Holocaust is one of a group of genocides that are linked by the struggles of the survivors to retain an awareness of a catastrophic event that remains, by its very nature, outside of linear progressive history, or, as Theodor Adorno put it, the "entire Western philosophical episteme." The descendants of those who perished in the Middle Passage, the Native American and Armenian genocides, and the Holocaust all share a struggle against historical amnesia on the part of the dominant culture. Hitler's comment to his generals in justifying the Holocaust, "Who, after all, speaks today of the annihilation of the Armenians?"[15] expresses all too clearly the danger of social amnesia. By apparently placing The Rich Jew in a separate category, *Garbage, The City and Death* represented for the Jewish community in Frankfurt a return to the type of thinking that creates genocide in the first place, and their protest must be seen in light of these historical conditions.

The Federal Republic's conservatives attacked the play as well. This polemic against the play, however, seems somewhat more suspect than the Jewish one. The Right, perhaps recognizing Fassbinder's critique of capitalism, took up the Jewish cause in a thinly veiled effort to lambaste Fassbinder's politics. During the attempt to stage the play in Frankfurt in 1985, the Right, led by the Frankfurter Allgemeine Zeitung, allied itself with the Jewish community against the Left, who tended to support production. Unfortunately, the Right's alliance, coming a year after the Bitburg incident—in which U.S. president Ronald Reagan honored the graves of S.S. officers but refused to pay homage to victims of the Holocaust—was not very convincing. During Reagan's visit to Bitburg, the Zeitung had in effect warned the Jews not to protest, for they would only be pressing their welcome in Germany.[16] Indeed, that whole episode, including Reagan's visit to the graves of the S.S., seemed to confirm the very anti-Semitism the Jews feared from Fassbinder.[17]

The conservative newspapers' disgust with *Garbage, The City and Death* seems more easily explained both because of Fassbinder's political convictions and defiant homosexuality and because the play, rather than simply blaming the Jews as the cause of German misery, actually implicates the capitalist mechanism as well as the subliminal fascistic tendencies present in every economic and social relationship. With the Right invested in denying the existence of fascism and national socialism for a variety of reasons, not the least being that many conservative industrialists were business partners of ranking Nazi officials, their insistent attack on *Garbage, The City and Death* seems merely to mask their anxiety over the notion that big business is complicit with institutionalized fascism.

In addition to these two views stood the political Left's response. The Left argued that no group, including the Jews, is singled out in the play, and that, even if The Rich Jew is an offensive character, the Jews are themselves not above criticism. This position seems suspect because the Jewish condition in Germany is not the same as that of other minority groups. While certainly they are not the only oppressed minority, the events of fifty years ago belong to a qualitatively different level of oppression from what others have experienced. To be Jewish in Germany in the 1930s and 1940s meant almost certain death, and collapsing that reality into a universal experience is historically irresponsible. Also, the Left insisted that, right or wrong, Fassbinder is entitled to his point of view. Reading the play in terms of "freedom of speech" also seems inadequate, however, for that rhetoric also avoids the fascism and anti-Semitism underlying Frankfurt society.

The three views above—Jewish, conservative, and Leftist—are the predominant responses to the play. Indeed, very few people have been willing to read it as anything other than an example of Fassbinder's own personal anti-Semitism, a reading that, in my opinion, misses the subtlety of Fassbinder's position on fascism. I hope to show that reading *Garbage, The City and Death* as an indictment of late capitalism and the fascistic underpinnings of everyday life, given Fassbinder's situation at the time, his avowed "politics of ambiguity" and interest in allegory, is a more useful approach. Along these lines, Heiner Müller notes that:

> Fassbinder's *Garbage, The City and Death* uses a victim's revenge to describe the devastation of a city in huge, harsh images. . . . The perversion of human relationships through their commodity character demonstrates a Biblical piece of wisdom: that the first fratricide, Cain, was also the first to establish a city. (1984a, 10)

Garbage, The City and Death comes immediately out of Fassbinder's experience of the Federal Republic, and Frankfurt in particular, during the 1970s. Not only do the contextual circumstances of *Garbage, The City and Death* reflect his understanding, but the textual apparatus designates a fascism that devastates human agency. Fassbinder's own political ambiguity in the play actually serves a particularly precise purpose: to implicate a much wider circle than that of the playtext. "There are anti-Semites in this play. But then they exist in other places too—in Frankfurt for instance" (Fassbinder 1976, 36).

Fassbinder's understanding of the effects of fascism on the social and political landscape of the play responds in part to the condition that Lyotard argues is covered by the differend. In the philosophical space that Lyotard labels "after Auschwitz," that is, after the realization of a model that is not reconcilable with transhistorical, or "dialectical," thinking, speculative discourse falters. Consequently, the premises of "justice" or "equality" are also suspended, as is the tacit agreement between "addressor" and "addressee" (speaker and listener) that implies a commonality of purpose.[18] In the "after Auschwitz" model, value is hard, if not impossible, to define. Yet Fassbinder does not simply throw his characters willy-nilly into a value-free, polylogical space. By recognizing the philosophical impasse in accounting for German anti-Semitism and focusing instead on the effects of capitalism on a world that includes anti-Semitism, Fassbinder confronts anti-Semitism not as a philosophical or moral issue but, instead, as a pattern of thought whose effects result in a particular historical sociopolitical configuration.[19]

The question of anti-Semitism in *Garbage, The City and Death*—a question that could also be asked about misogyny, racism, or homophobia—is part of the political nihilism and indeed of the particular model of simulation that the play proposes. "Simulation designates the power of producing an *effect*. But this is not only in a causal sense, because causality would remain completely hypothetical and indeterminate without the intervention of other meanings" (Deleuze 1990, 263). Certainly The Rich Jew served a political purpose in Frankfurt's reception of *Garbage, The City and Death*. The character's universality dragged the Frankfurt community into a confrontation with its own anti-Semitism. If anything, the sociopolitical weight of what anti-Semitism and/or fascism means to Germany, and to State capitalism, decrees that any effort to implicate such sentiments through individual characters, through the creation of a notion of individual agency as an explanation for participation in such structures, is to depoliticize an event such as the Holocaust. Andreas Huyssen identifies a primary structure in "Auschwitz" as one that declares null the concern with individuality that has defined European thought since the Enlightenment: "The enormity of Auschwitz itself forbids emotional identification with individual victims. This is what Adorno had in mind when he criticized the Anne Frank play for focusing on an individual victim which consequently permitted the audience to forget the whole" (110). If disabusing characters of their "humanistic" traits, such as compassion or love—the universals by which Platonism distinguishes between good and bad copies—turns them into simulacra, they are also able to lose the characteristics that would fix them within the specificity humanism utilizes to depoliticize its constituents. As simulacra without moral or ethical imperatives, they can attack the foundations of humanist discourse. The text's nihilism and attendant anti-Semitism, racism, and misogyny become not only individual traits but also structural components of the society in which *Garbage, The City and Death* takes place. Of course, situating anti-Semitism in this way does not make the individuals involved any less culpable, nor does it make Fassbinder any less complicit. However, what the play does do is expose the processes by which fascistic relationships are internalized and consequently normativized in capitalist society.

Placing these hypercharacters among clearly recognizable cultural artifacts (e.g., *La Traviata*, and designating them as prostitutes, pimps, homosexuals, rich Jews) establishes them as tropes within the framework of a discursive milieu—specifically, the economic terrain of Frankfurt. Without the humanist specificity of clearly identifiable individuals, they can roam through the play undermining the illusionism of the "theological stage."

As simulacra, they push the stakes of discourse to a point at which the dwarf's delirious melodrama can sound like "everyday life," an intensification that ultimately precludes the recuperation of these characteristics to a normativizing discourse. "The secret is to oppose to the order of the real an absolutely imaginary realm . . . whose implosive energy absorbs everything real and all the violence of real power which founders there" (Baudrillard 1982, 119). Fassbinder's play is a form of political terrorism whose grenades are simulacra and whose hostages are the humanist discourses that subtend fascism into respectability. Yet no attempt is made in the play to redeem these hostages. These simulacra both expose and destroy the basis of Platonic discourse, leaving in its stead a nihilistic vacuum, and also potentiate a new possibility for liberation from Platonism—a freedom that, while unexplored in the play itself, must start with the rise of the simulacrum, and that first requires the defounding of any sort of humanism. Here, too, is where Fassbinder's work obtains its critique of anti-Semitism. By focusing on the political and economic underpinnings of fascism and capitalism, the text refuses to categorize anti-Semitism as an event separate from its socioeconomic context. At the same time, Fassbinder does not seek to appropriate the experience of the Holocaust to a humanist master-narrative by incorporating into his own experience.[20] Instead, the play places anti-Semitism at an allegorical level, one in which its complicity with capitalism can be clearly understood.

The difference between Foreman's and Fassbinder's texts is similar to the difference between the masquerade for/of the father (pretending that the father, and not writing, is behind the staged word) and the simulacrum. The difference renders subjects and objects as well as their attendant economies (economies predicated on transcendental signifiers) inarticulate, by problematizing the position from which they would otherwise speak. Where the characters in *Garbage, The City and Death* descend into the imploded fascistic universe imagined by Baudrillard, Phoebe and her colleagues become hyperreal. Not a hysterical nostalgia for an origin, but a hyperreality of forces that are deterritorialized and allowed to form their own affinities (though the optimism of such a statement is problematic). For if, following Deleuze rather than Baudrillard, the simulacrum rather than the "real" predicates the theatrical economy of the word, the ensuing hyperreality results as a liberative affirmation that allows an all-out assault on the "real" that need not entail either falling away from the ideal or imploding the social sphere. The terrain constituted by Fassbinder's plays imparts a radically different sphere of theatricality from that which the "theological" conception of theater would allow. If this stage is still dominated by words and their attendant hierarchy of father/son economies, even as it reaches the Theatre of Cruelty, then it is a theology wherein the god has long since died, and no amount of ideation can revive him nor keep the reveling simulacra from dancing on his grave.

In fact, it would not even be possible to talk about Fassbinder's theater in metaphysical terms were it not still tied to the word. While this theater effects a radical perturbation of the metaphysic of "the father," it does not exist outside that economy. Like Phoebe Zeitgeist, it is a theater of the transgressed limit. Fassbinder's characters are worse than bad sons running about murderously and unchecked. They perch on the borders of the representational framework, speaking out of its elided positions. They do not stand in for nor masquerade as the father, do not fill in for him through the playwright's words nor enact through their deeds his absent presence. They violently destroy the framework that constitutes fathers and sons.

What questions do these characters raise about the representational framework and the theatrical enterprise? The strategies Fassbinder employs in his attack on metaphysics and representation apparently reach the limit of the stage, a limit whose transgression would either signal the end of theater or facilitate a slide back into the territory of the frame. Fassbinder brings anarchy to the stage with no interest in controlling its effects, providing an escape from representation, or leaving intact his own position. The nihilism his characters evince would seemingly suggest a traditional analysis of their condition (their torpid state is a tragic result of alienation and the bankruptcy of humanistic values). Rather than finding cause for sorrow within that position, however, they instead use it to "off" the residuals of their theological heritage. The merciless textuality these characters designate seemingly leaves no room for the reinsertion of an ego such as Foreman's, for identity in the world of Phoebe Zeitgeist or Roma B. is possible only as self-delusion, the consequences of which are apparently articulated in and as fascism. What Fassbinder provides in wasting the theological frame of representation is an opportunity for performing a reformulation of character and identity along a nonfascistic genealogy.

Indeed, by fixating on freeing the stage from its "false copies," that is, by attempting to reconstruct the apparatus of the stage without problematizing the foundations on which its traditional conventions are predicated, Foreman cannot address his own culpability in representation and remains, even when it falls to pieces, under the sway of the Same. His intense concentration on the formal elements of his work, even though developed in a historical context in which such rhetorical practices were radical, limits deconstruction by losing sight of the ideological constructs within the work. Foreman's wit and subtlety of observation are undeniable, but they mask his recuperation of the position of the father in his texts. Through exploring the simulacrum, Fassbinder, Deleuze, Irigaray, and Derrida perturb the process of theological hierarchization and make way for a creative chaos whose end is the destruction of Platonism. While practicing similar textual disassemblages as those Foreman begins with, they make no effort at reterritorializing the stage toward an ideal. The *écriture* of simulacra becomes one of anarchy, in which the possibility for a repressive recuperation is always a possibility but by no means a given. Indeed, the simulacrum could lead toward a liberative textuality, one not recuperable to a master-narrative teleology. Yet, as Baudrillard relentlessly shows, the cynicism underlying the simulacrum must not be underestimated. To paraphrase Aristotle, the confrontation between Fassbinder and Foreman suggests, finally, that Foreman sees people as they should be and Fassbinder as they are. Between ideation and actuality, then, there lies a world of *différance*.

CHAPTER 3

In Homini Memoriam: Caryl Churchill, Wallace Shawn, Kathy Acker, and the Ends of Man

Why do we so carefully, so resolutely, deny this "inexorable affirmation"? Why do we prefer the certainty of death to the "impossibility of dying"? Aesthetic idealization is perhaps best defined as a will-to-death, a refusal at once of living and of dying.

—Steven Shaviro, *Passion and Excess*

Life in this society being, at best, an utter bore and no aspect of society being at all relevant to women, there remains to civic-minded, responsible, thrill-seeking females only to overthrow the government, eliminate the money system, institute complete automation and destroy the male sex.

—Valerie Solanis

The aim of critique is not the end of reason or the end of man but in the end the Overman, the overcome, overtaken man. This point of critique is not justification but a different way of feeling: another sensibility.

—Gilles Deleuze, *Nietzsche and Philosophy*

Caryl Churchill's *Softcops*, Wallace Shawn's *A Thought in Three Parts*, and Kathy Acker's *The Birth of the Poet* focus on notions of the body, sex, and the "ends of Man." These plays also exemplify problems in humanism that Shaviro and Solanis suggest are in part responsible for a world that creates not freedom and happiness but, instead, systems of domination. The central trope activated by these plays is that of "Man," the concrete universal. Through a critique of humanism's apparatus and operational modes, these plays set the stage for an Other sensibility that exemplifies the difference between the man who is indeed an utter bore and of no relevance at all except as another instance of power and the overcome Man who can no longer justify humanism and who is, in fact, pushed aside by the appearance of "other sensibilities."

In the previous chapter, I suggested that Foreman's and Fassbinder's plays disrupt the closure of representation by assaulting its framework from the "margin" of that frame. In doing so, they expose the hyperreality of representations of "the real." Yet neither set of plays subverts representation per se. While Phoebe Zeitgeist can assert the contingency of meanings and discourse and the displacement of authority by indeterminacy with a "playfulness" that has almost nothing to do with fun, neither she nor the plays in which her "spirit" appears transgress the law she and they are bound by, for they cannot do away with representation. Indeed, recent schools of thought have repeatedly stressed the limit and limitations of "transgression" sui generis. Might there be other options, however, other possibilities for contesting the power of representation to structure discourse? Could theater, or theatricality, envision an incipient sensibility that resides "in the realm of the senseless" (the title of one of Kathy Acker's novels) that both resists and creates, one that completes Deleuze's notion of the simulacrum?

Yet even that notion is too simplistic, too optimistic, to invoke without first mapping the terrain on which it could materialize. The claims of humanism—that the self is knowable, representable, and of importance to the world at large and, furthermore, that these claims are something shared by "all men"—disguise the actual mechanisms and interests of the societies that have fallen under the sway of a science designed to "know thyself." The effect of the institutionalization of knowledge has been to produce a set or series of discourses that both impel certain normative behaviors to dominate the realm of the senses and, further, to designate behavior that falls outside of a "normative" pattern as "deviant" or "criminal" and thus to restrict or prohibit them in a manner in which their restriction and prohibition appear entirely "natural." Foucault's famous image, at the end of *The Order of Things*, summarizes a certain post-structural attitude toward humanism: "If those arrangements were to disappear as they appeared, if some event of which we can at the moment do no more than sense the possibility . . . were to cause them to crumble, . . . then one can certainly wager that man would be erased, like a face drawn in sand at the edge of the sea" (1970, 387).

A critique of modernism and humanism sets the stage, so to speak, for much of post-structuralist thought. While this critique has implications that range far beyond the scope of this project, it is useful to point out that the notions of a "world spirit," of "transcendental subjectivity," and of progressive history have come to be understood in the last twenty years as tropes for the operations of a power/knowledge nexus. Consequently, when these tropes become understood as political, humanism's moment is over. Humanism has become a danger to culture; a simple litany of the excesses of the twentieth century in the name of "progress" and "evolution" should suffice to suggest where and how its failures have been most apparent. Peter Sloterdijk suggests that all that can be expected from humanism at this point in history is "a subjectivity without a subject, which, if thought out further as a general principle, cannot produce anything more than a postmodern colloquium, entitled: 'The Autumn Salon of the Vanities, upon Which Intensities Collapse into Each Other, in a Manner That is Guaranteed to Be Meaning-Free and Polylogical'" (74). Once it becomes apparent that knowledge, subjectivity, or agency are in fact discursive functions, their claim to universality is suspended. This does not mean, however, that the constructions of humanism are not still dominant today, even though it is also necessary to view these humanisms, at least in the theater, as failures, for they have not provided their constituency with the sort of transcendental individualism that they promised.

With the critique of humanism in mind, I attempt in this chapter to explore the boundaries of two "limit-texts"—the body and sex—and how those boundaries structure discourse as a prison with specific reference to *Softcops* and *A Thought in Three Parts*. Then, based on the critique developed through reading the first two plays, I suggest how in *The Birth of the Poet* "other sensibilities" appear after the "end of Man." The deployment of power causes the body and sex to be subsumed by discourse and thus reproduced as aspects of power relations rather than as "naturally" occurring phenomena. These three plays investigate power's relationship to the body and sex as well as attempts to problematize those effects. Not that the plays provide answers, or "the truth." Rather, they exemplify the connections between language, knowledge, and power and suggest that the site on which these discourses play out is the body. In these plays, the body is not a naturally occurring object but, instead, is constructed through and in language, thus creating an inextricable connection between the body, language, and sexuality. The manner in which the body is constituted is a major element in these plays: "The body in question is not a 'natural' body but rather the sexual body that speaks. Language intersects with the body and cuts through it; language constitutes it as a speaking body, while the speaking body in turn marks language with its irreducible sexuality" (Nägele 75). Rainer Nägele emphasizes the political stakes of language for the body and for sexuality by drawing attention to the relationship of language and the body, a relationship that, in determining how the body is represented and constructed, affects what meanings it is given.

Churchill wrote her play in response to Foucault's problematization of the human sciences as a legitimating discourse. By replaying issues around the establishment of the prison, *Softcops* records the shift in effects of power on the body as notions of discipline and punishment change historically. *Softcops* analyzes the "soft" methods of social control so important to the current *epistème:* "There is a constant attempt by governments to depoliticize illegal acts, to make criminals a separate class from the rest of society so that subversion will not be general, and part of this process is the invention of the detective and the criminal, the cop and the robber" (Churchill 3). The play mirrors the structure of Foucault's *Discipline and Punish*, in which he sought to write a history of punishment in order to understand how the body has been, and still is, used as a technology of power: "Thus . . . one might understand both how man, the soul, the normal or abnormal individual have come to duplicate crime as objects of penal intervention; and in what way a specific mode of subjection was able to give birth to man as an object of knowledge for a discourse with a 'scientific' status" (Foucault 1979, 24).

Foucault suggests that the actual practices of disciplining and punishing the body, of making the body conform and of normativizing its functions and activities, mark a paradigmatic deployment of power and contribute substantially as discursive modes to the constitution of a society. This notion of the deployment of bodies as functional constituents of State apparatus is the leaping-off point for *Softcops*. Churchill states in her introduction: "I had had an idea for a play . . . which was to be about the soft methods of control, schools, hospitals, social workers, when I came across the Foucault book (*Discipline and Punish*), and was so thrilled with it that I set the play not here and now but in Nineteenth Century France" (6). The play presents three men (the play's all male cast is significant in Churchill's oeuvre), each of whom has different notions of how to discipline and punish "criminals." The Minister believes in corporal punishment: public displays of torture and slow execution that purify the body politic by expunging its criminal elements. His public displays of horrific punishments—drawing and quartering, burning, breaking on the wheel—will cower the populace into behaving. He is opposed by Pierre, who wishes to build an "English garden" of punishment. Its crowning feature will be a cage suspending the most infamous criminal, the parricide, between heaven and earth. In this garden, the individual citizen can view various stations of punishment in private and thus reflect on his or her own status and on the consequences of abandoning the public interest for a life of crime. Finally, there is Vidocq, the master criminal, who, once installed as chief of police, creates a regime of observation in which every criminal is watched and interceded with before he or she can do wrong. By so doing, Vidocq (who is based on an actual historical figure) hopes to prevent criminals from acting, because they will always be within the gaze of the panopticon, their every thought and movement watched, marked, and cataloged. *Softcops* reflects the trajectory examined in *Discipline and Punish* of the historical development of attitudes toward punishment and the body by following the historical development of observation versus annihilation and showing the mechanisms by which these systems are socially installed. By emphasizing the fundamentally historical aspects of these processes, the characters trace a shift in the social topology of Western society: a shift from public bodies contractually related to the "king" to private bodies whose subjectivity is a result of an institutionalized power apparatus legitimated by the State.

Softcops translates Foucault's triadic structure of the history of incarceration into a one generational time frame. While *Discipline and Punish* analyzes a historical period of roughly 150 years—from the public dismemberment and torture of a regicide through the internalization of controls to the isolating omnipresent gaze—*Softcops* condenses the shift into approximately one decade. The play is set in France in the 1830s, yet no specific time progression is stipulated. Instead, the play presents the struggle between three views on punishment, their respective effects on both criminals and legislatures, and, finally, the triumph of the panoptic gaze as an internalized instrument of repression and control that needs only minor coercive enforcement, that is, enforcement at an individual level. Each of the eleven scenes shows various effects of certain forms of incarceration. The first scenes concern the earliest method of discipline and punishment: public torture and execution. In front of a band of schoolchildren, a thief's hand is chopped off, and a murderer is to be hanged. Unfortunately for the attendant minister and his deputies, the murderer's irreverent last words incite the crowd to riot; the murderer and the executioner are mobbed, and soldiers must be called in to restore public order.

The middle section of the play shows the installation of an internal system that controls subversive behavior through fear and paranoia, and the depoliticization of criminal acts. Vidocq, a former criminal who is appointed chief of police by the Minister, forms a secret police force to monitor and control the actions of such subversives as a bank robber and a revolutionary. As part of his subterfuge, Vidocq allows an imprisoned thief-murderer to circulate his writings and poetry. Through his fictitious accounts of his own criminal exploits, Lacenaire the prisoner becomes a cause célèbre among the bourgeoisie and literati for exhibiting a romantic (yet failed—he is in jail) criminality. Lacenaire's thievery, rather than being punished as an attack on the rich by the poor, is turned into a literary feat, accessible to the bourgeoisie only as the prototypical detective story. Unlike the earlier public torture, in which the populace could clearly distinguish between the ruling class and the people, Lacenaire's writings turn crime into a personal matter that is in no way linked to politics. Lacenaire is created by the police as a hero-criminal who displays the attributes of the emergent class in such a way that he justifies the police's existence. By isolating the criminal, and criminality, and by romanticizing crime (historically, detective novels and magazines became popular during this period), the existence of a police force is justified within the domain of a bourgeois social order. A second example of the success of Vidocq's internalization of social control is when an undercover policeman posing as a worker arrests a revolutionary who is agitating for food for the workers.

The final section completes the progression of soft, or internal, controls. A deviant youth learns that, to avoid punishment in a reform school, he must control himself; a revolutionary is sold out by an informer to the police; finally, a group of prisoners at the seaside need only an occasional beating to keep them docile and obedient. These three scenarios establish the gaze that Jeremy Bentham's panopticon made possible. The criminals and deviants are controlled through surveillance by an omnipotent authority that manifests in the most mundane forms and individualized according to a behavioral norm. The architecture of the prison becomes the architecture of society; the discipline and surveillance of the body constructs a social space dedicated to internalized, self-regulatory systems. *Softcops* plots the trajectory of the body's gradual absorption by discursive order. From the raw impulses of nature to the disciplined and docile norms of a social order dependent on large numbers of autonomous workers, in Churchill's play the body is the ground on which these controls are effected. At issue here is the degree of autonomy, or self-volition, any subject has at any given historical moment.

The shift from public to private regulation of bodies represents a social cartology based not on the classical position of the king, not on a mode of hierarchical, and fixed, positions, but, instead, on a relational mode wherein certain forces attain precedence over others according to the exigencies of the particular dominant order. Furthermore, this relational social order appeared historically at the moment of the emergence of the bourgeoisie and of early capitalism. By replacing the external figure of the king with the internal figure of a private self, the emergent social and political orders were able to dictate a system of values conducive to private ownership, to mercantile systems, and to the subjection of the body to the needs of economic systems based on the premise of rational, objective knowledge.[1] The body thus becomes an object for those systems, separated from the self and available for economic exploitation.

Consequently, punishment becomes a method of social control: "Punishment was seen as a technique for the coercion of individuals; it operated methods of training the body—not signs—by the traces it leaves, in the form of habits, in behavior; and it presupposed the setting up of a specific power for the administration of the penalty" (Foucault 1979, 131). As with the dissolution of truth as a metaphysical conceit, the ordering of bodies follows a similar decentering, a privatization, that coterminously entails a rupture in the value of the body. "The body, required to be docile in its minutest operations, opposes and shows the conditions of functioning proper to an organism. Disciplinary power has as its correlative an individuality that is not only analytical and 'cellular,' but also natural and 'organic'" (156). Whereas once a regicide might be tortured in the most grotesque display of mortification, now the crime itself is circumvented by containing and normativizing any and all possible actions; by the formation of "docile bodies" that are contained and controlled like bit players in "so many small theaters, in which each actor is alone, perfectly individualized and constantly visible" (200).[2] Clearly, in terms of the stakes of the naturalization and internalization of control, it would seem that this privatization entails the adoption of a society based on what Althusser calls the "ideological state apparatus."

As Pierre stumbles through his proposed speech at the end of *Softcops*, the end of the body as a primary, unified signifier is projected:

> *Pierre:* I shall just explain quite simply how the criminals are punished, the sick are cured, the workers are supervised, the ignorant are educated, the unemployed are registered, the insane are normalized. The criminals—No wait a minute. The criminals are supervised, the insane are cured. . . . No. I'll need to re-

hearse this a little. The ignorant are normalized. Right. . . . The insane are educated, the workers are cured. The unemployed are punished. The criminals are normalized. Something along those lines. (28)

Pierre finally articulates a system of containment that depoliticizes every act and that segments society into a series of norms. What is incredible in his stuttering seaside speech, composed as one of the guards shoots a prisoner whom he is supposed to be guarding, is the extent to which the incarceration of the prisoners into criminality is a result of Pierre's struggle with language, with the discursivity of power. It is a struggle, furthermore, that composes criminality not as an isolated act but, rather, as a reaction to normativized behavior.

> *Pierre:* He stirred up trouble at his place of work. Something about an association of workers. He resisted the police to such an extent the army had to be called in. Extremely violent criminal type, psychopath, paranoid fantasies, unhappy childhood, alcoholic father, inadequate mother. . . . Extremely disorganized personality, with high blood pressure and low intelligence, a weak heart, anarchist literature, abnormal sexual proclivities, and cold feet due to inadequate circulation. (47)

The list of causes has nothing to do with the worker's dissatisfaction with capitalism, for example. Instead his behavior is broken down and subjected to classification in terms of a norm that absolves society from responsibility. The inability of the worker to discipline his body and sexuality to the norms required by his industrialized society must be contained precisely because, without that control, the worker meanders on a selvage that threatens the reproductive codes necessary to fulfill industrial capitalism's labor needs.[3]

The discursive grid that Pierre composes creates an entire field of experts and disciplines to establish and police useful behaviors as well as incriminate excess or anarchy and expunge it as beyond the pale. "Hence the major effect of the Panopticon: To induce in the inmate a state of conscious and permanent visibility that assures the automatic function of power" (Foucault 1979, 201). Bentham's Panopticon is a visual model of discipline that not only arranges bodies spatially but, also, when combined with the historically coterminous emergence of sexuality as a representable mode, effects a discourse of marked bodies and sexuality as ideological progenitors of power. "The society that emerged in the nineteenth century . . . did not confront sex with a fundamental refusal of recognition. On the contrary, it put into operation an entire machinery for producing true discourses concerning it" (Foucault 1980a, 69). For Churchill to translate a theory onto a body, a project central to all her plays, is to localize the contestation of force relationships—to interiorize within the domain of power, and thus politics, the processes of subjectification. This is the role of the "soul" that, for Foucault, becomes the operational matrix of power:

> This real, non-corporal soul is not a substance; it is the element in which are articulated the effects of a certain type of power, and the reference of a certain type of knowledge, the machinery by which the power relations give rise to a possible corpus of knowledge, and knowledge extends and reinforces the effects of this power. (29)

Rather than resorting to the sort of physical punishment that Pierre and the Minister hope for, Vidocq demonstrates that it is easier to initiate control internally, so that individuals are responsible for their own restraint. Of course, the objection could be raised that *Softcops* localizes its processes too much, that assigning a name (rigid designator) and, consequently, agency (exteriority) to these individuals imbues them with too much responsibility for the constitution of discourse. As such, they are agents capable of producing discourse rather than the products of social relations. Indeed, positing these characters as outside of discourse plays well into the interests of ideological State apparatus, for it constitutes their actions in terms of the individual's needs or desires and thus suggests that different men would have acted differently and, thus, that the individual is somehow capable of determining his or her own outcome.

Yet that would be a misreading of Churchill's play, for neither

Vidocq, the Minister, or Pierre function simply as individuals with pasts, presents, or futures within a realistic play but, instead, are bit players in a discursive struggle for control of the body within its cultural context. Consequently, rather than subjects imbued with agency, or representations of such, they are tropes constituting three versions of relations, three *epistèmes* who coalesce within a representational, panoptic space. At the same time, however, in the theatrical economy (and in the history provided by "Foucault"), they are real characters, with the lives and interests that that "real" implies within that economy, and the play follows a more or less realistic arc. By including with these realist characters their own critique, by showing their actions and linking those actions to the characters' societal positions, the play reveals the social structures of discipline and the mechanisms with which bodies are manipulated within a field. By presenting both sides of the picture, so to speak, the private lives of the characters along with their discursive functions, *Softcops* shows the complexity of social formations. It is not enough to simply critique a social position without also imbricating any position of critique with that social position as well.

Softcops posits three points in configuring a notion of resistance to the body's incarceration into discourse, given that any such strategies can only imagine, not actually situate, a realm outside the panopticism of power. First, Pierre's stuttering in his final speech suggests that the normativization of criminals, the insane, and workers does not occur as a consequence of an impersonal fate but, rather, as a function of the interests of a particular social class.

> If there is an overall political issue around the prison, it is not therefore whether it is to be corrective or not; whether the judges, the psychiatrists or the sociologists are to exercise more power in it than the administrators or supervisors; it is not even whether we should have prison or something other than prison. At present, the problem lies rather in the steep rise in the use of these mechanisms of normalization and the wide-ranging powers which, through the proliferation of new disciplines, they bring with them. (Foucault 1979, 306)

In order to legitimate the structure of incarceration, it must be linked directly to a structuration of norms. The second point raised in *Softcops* concerns the social need for criminality. Without it, the repressive State apparatus (the police) would have no reason to exist: "No crime means no police. What makes the presence and control of the police tolerable for the population, if not fear of the criminal?" (Foucault 1980b, 47). In similar manner to how madness and civilization are created, that is, in the institutionalizing of discourses with which to talk of norms and deviance, criminality can be used to maintain a docile population and the need for a police state, simply as the negative consequence of a notion of "the good."

Softcops investigates the contingencies of the social formation that designate certain actions as "criminal" or "acceptable." Indeed, the play emphasizes that these contingencies are the result of an interplay of forces that are manipulated to serve certain social functions. "The panoptic mechanism is not simply a hinge, a point of exchange between a mechanism of power and a function; it is a way of making power relations functions in a function, and of making a function through these power relations" (Foucault 1979, 206–7). Consequently, there is always something at stake in the operation of a State apparatus, always something that can be lost or can escape, something that must be contained in order for the apparatus to maintain itself:

> The carceral . . . communicates a type of power that the law validates and that justice uses as its favorite weapon. How could the disciplines and the power that functions in them appear arbitrary, when they merely operate the mechanisms of justice itself . . . carceral continuity and the fusion of the prison-form make it possible to legalize, or in any case to legitimate, disciplinary power. (302)

Historically, the inception of a system of panoptic restraints did not reduce or remove the "criminal element" but actually made it more apparent, more clearly defined its operations and the boundaries through which it attained a definition. "The carceral pyramid gives to the power to inflict legal punishment a context in which it appears to be free of all excess and all violence" (302). Indeed, this continuation of a struggle between forces, between the norm and the deviant, the inside and the outside wherein the one must more rigidly fortify itself against the Other, led Foucault to ask whether the history of discipline and punishment should be written as a success or whether, in fact, in the final analysis, it is actually a history of failure. In this light, Pierre's stutterings at the end of the play are more than just the establishment of a control grid over the body; they are also an example of how this grid itself is contestable, if only in a post-apocalyptic world such as that which constitutes Acker's *The Birth of the Poet*. If so, then the continued search for new and more efficient models of incarceration and containment can be seen as an active and prolonged struggle against the outside, against what the State apparatus cannot contain.

The self/body is repressed not only through institutionalized violence. One of the central notions in Wallace Shawn's *A Thought in Three Parts* is that sexual behavior has been consumed by sexuality as a discursive regulator; that is, where sex might once have been an *ars erotica*, a source of pleasure, it becomes, through the establishment of a *Scientia Sexualis*, an imperative to know, a discursive artifact. In fact, Foucault has argued that, over the past three hundred years, both the body and sex have become subsumed by institutionalized discourses whose major engine is power. Thus, rather than being the experience or enactment of sex, sexuality becomes the processing of sociopolitical power relations played out on the terrain of the (gendered) body. It is also made to seek its own repression, to comport normative modes of behavior and remain within narrow confines of acceptability. Wallace Shawn's play documents a particular version of the use and function of sexuality in contemporary white middle-class society. In *A Thought in Three Parts*, sexuality becomes a technology for the functioning of power and, consequently, for the functioning of knowledge, a nexus of forces (power/knowledge, a critical nexus in a society predicated in part on the Platonic "knowledge is virtue" ethos) that describes the actual, material effects of language as power.[4] As indicated by the title, the play is organized in three sections, yet the relation between the three parts seems tangential at best. No character appears in more than one section, and the scenarios for each do not appear to be related; the only apparent narrative through-line is that the characters in each section discuss sex, albeit in different ways. David and Sarah, the two characters in the first part, "Summer Evening," carry on a conversation in their foreign hotel room. They speak "very fast, much faster than people really speak" (31). Their conversation is also without pauses, as if they were talking over, as much as to, each other. They talk about life in the hotel, food, clothing, sleep, and, most important, their relationship. They experience a certain dis-ease, or dissatisfaction, with each other:

> *Sarah:* I don't like this book. I hate it. I'm sorry.
> *David:* —don't like it?—
> *Sarah:* —not funny, it's dirty—I hate it.
> *David:* I'm sorry.
> *Sarah:* Well it's not your fault—
> *David:* Well it is, I'm sure.
> *Sarah:* Well I really don't think so. (36)

Sarah expresses her dissatisfaction with David:

> *Sarah:* Do you know what love means?
> *David:* Well—
> *Sarah:* Or are you actually only a little piece of shit, who's learned how to *talk* about feelings?
> *David:* Well I *feel* that I'm not— (40)

Then the situation reverses, and David rejects Sarah:

> *Sarah:* David?
> *David:* Yes?
> *Sarah:* Will you leave me tonight, darling?
> *David:* Tonight? What? Will I leave you *tonight*? Here's a book I

don't feel like reading. Here's one I don't feel like. Here's one I don't think that I—God, do you hear those sounds? (41)

Through their constant bickering, the question emerges whether they can be emotionally compatible or whether one or the other is merely an amusement, a plaything in place of a nurturing relationship. By the end of the section, they seem to have worked out their differences, for David turns off the light and begins to make love to Sarah.

David: —stems—pale leaves—
Sarah: —just the light from outside. *(He touches a switch on the night table, and the lights of the room go out.)* Yes. *(They touch.)* Yes.
David: May I?
Sarah: Yes. (41)

In "Summer Evening," sexuality appears everywhere except in sex. The couple never touch until the end, when the lights are out. Instead, they play a game of deferral, posing and posturing as a couple bound to a social contract that designates certain behaviors but without ever actually engaging in sex. On the surface, David and Sarah's onstage sexless activities fall entirely within a "normal" bourgeois theater discourse. But, taking into account the stage direction— "[they] speak very fast, much faster than people really speak. They almost never leave pauses between their lines, so that their dialogue is almost overlapping" (31)—and the actions of the section that follows, "Youth Hostel," their conversations upset the normative social function of their mundane conversation. By speeding up the dialogue, and by juxtaposing the scene's apparent normalcy to the following scene's sexual abandon, the scene's bourgeois context is bracketed and its assumptions temporarily suspended.

If physical sex is concealed or elided by a discursive sexuality in "Summer Evening," in the next part, "Youth Hostel," sex is everywhere onstage except in sexuality. The section is a lurid overdose of sex divorced from any emotional interactions. The four characters, Judy, Dick, Helen, and Bob, fornicate and masturbate themselves and one another not with passionate abandon but, rather, with a clinical precision that, despite the intensity of any one episode, immediately reduces the experience to a banality completely opposite to David and Sarah's rhapsodic mating games. The climactic finale of "Summer Evening" is couched in obliquely poetic language:

> *Sarah:* I once put a silver coin on my tongue. Do you know? Then I dried, I was dripping with sweat . . . the coin was an eye. I was watching the ocean. . . . It was white, it was burning . . . the water was twisting in pain.
> *David:* Now, it's night, there are stars, there are clouds, and they're racing in the sky . . . at the end there's a stream, and I lay you down in it and wash you. (40–41)

Unlike David's fantasy about making love to a dead Sarah, a fantasy resonant with misogynist sexuality, the escapades in "Youth Hostel" bypass any such sublimation for an immediate experience:

> *Judy:* But what's the matter? Don't you feel like talking? I thought you'd be lonely.
> *Dick:* Oh Judy—I've been trying to be by myself for hours. Helen's been in here giving me a hard time.
> *Judy:* Oh—really? Here—Let me do it. (*She starts to jerk him off.*)
> *Dick:* No—Really—Judy—you don't need to.
> *Judy:* I want to—honestly, Dickie.
> *Dick:* I know, Judy, but—
> *Judy:* You don't want me to? Do you want to have me?
> *Dick:* No—I only—
> *Judy:* (*Pulling up her skirt.*) Look—here—here—let me get right on you. Oh—oh—you see?—wowee—(*She sits on him and they make love.*) Oh, boy—this is really enjoyable! Yes! Yes! (*She comes, then he immediately comes.*) Oh, gee—
> *Dick:* Yeah—I have to admit that felt awfully good, Judy. I'm glad you did it to me.
> *Judy:* Thanks Dick. (48)

The section contains so many such "French" scenes, including two-somes, threesomes, and foursomes, that the bounds of orgasmic endurance are well surpassed. Yet neither liberation nor a deeper understanding of "human" nature (Thanatos or Eros) comes, so to speak, through these acts. "To conceive the category of the sexual in terms of the law, death, blood and sovereignty—whatever the references to Sade and Bataille, and however one might gauge their 'subversive' influence—is in the last analysis a historical 'retroversion'" (Foucault 1980a, 150). Instead, by the end of the section, the four characters enter the same state of isolation, the same repressive dialectic with which they began:

> Suddenly all feel cold. Bob sneezes loudly, takes a blanket and wraps himself up. Judy enters Room 2 and lies down on the bed. She masturbates with difficulty, manually and with her pillow. Bob leans against a wall of Room 1 and shuts his eyes. Dick washes himself with some water in a corner of the room and finally lies down on the bed. Helen wraps herself in a blanket and gets some food from the big box. She eats it, huddled to the wall. All are shivering. Judy continues to masturbate. (52)

Despite the physical contact, none of them realizes any special truth. In the final scene of the section, Judy's husband, Tom, comes in, and they have a vicious argument about his inability to find a job. In fact, Tom beats Judy until he almost falls asleep, a seemingly routine occurrence:

> *Tom:* Your mouth is open, Judy.
> *Judy:* Do you really like me? Do you really like me?
> *Tom:* I know what it means Judy. Put on more makeup?
> *Judy:* "Here we finally are, Judy."
> *Tom:* Do you want to help me now? I could use a fuck.
> *Judy:* "I think I understand you, Judy." (*They sit for a long time. Both feel cold. Judy shudders. Silence.*) (55)

Whereas David and Sarah were able to move through a spoken discourse to a physical and emotional crescendo, Judy and the other four move from physical closeness to an emotional wasteland.

In the final section, "Mr. Frivolous," Mr. Frivolous, "a man in his thirties" (56), recollects a sexual experience from the previous night, yet one that he reflects not as a history but, rather, as an actual, tactile event. Unlike the physical sex of "Youth Hostel," "Mr. Frivolous" depicts a discursive sexuality that uses certain erotic and pornographic iconography in presenting the concealed sexual event. The event itself is not the only thing concealed. The identification of his lover as well as the distinction between what Mr. Frivolous remembers and what actually took place are both blurred in such a way that any sex in the section takes place on the surface level of language:

> *Mr. Frivolous:* To hold. To take. Me in. To hug on me. Hard. While I. Am Sliding. While I. Am Pressing. While the Hours. Pass. And our bodies get wet. (57)

Even the syntax changes to replicate the wet interflow of passion:

> *Mr. Frivolous:* I ask you to love. I ask you to love me. . . . And washed. And cleaned. And washed. And cleaned. I ask. I ask. I ask. I ask. For your arms. To be there. And your shoulders. There. And for you. To open. And for you. (57)

It is as if the anticipation and experience of sex translate into his speech patterns and, in doing so, allow the speech to displace the sexuality from the sex into a linguistic economy. An abbreviated sentence structure, however, is not the only device that accomplishes this transfer. The references to priests—

> *Mr. Frivolous:* Priest, Touch me. Priest, Father, I have asked you to come here, to tell you, these clothes of yours have stayed here with me too long. Lie down here beside me (57)

—to quasiromantic poetry—

> *Mr. Frivolous:* With wings unfurled, our angels scattered light across the grass (57)

—and domestic bliss—

> *Mr. Frivolous:* Then we gathered up our clothes . . . and headed for home, to wash, to dress, to have dinner, and then to bed, and tuck you in, and lights out (57)

—again pull the event he describes away from a physical act and into various sexual/social discourses. In doing so, the text designates and delimits certain normative behaviors that perforce raise questions of gender and sexual orientation, questions that the text finally makes no effort to answer.

Indeed, the final section of the text seems to perform the very task by which a normative discourse would insure its ascendancy. The norm in Western society enforces heterosexuality; other sexualities, however, are dealt with in a twofold manner. On the one hand, homosexuality, bisexuality, and polysexuality are carefully elided through a facade of acceptance and tolerance, a celebration of difference justified by the underlying that "we" are really all the same "underneath our" sexuality. By sanitizing sexuality as a part of a unified human experience, difference disappears along with sexuality. On the other hand, repression is transferred to an economic or social, rather than physical, level. While physical repression—assault, beatings, murder—certainly still occurs, from the point of institutional power such behavior is designated as "nonnormative" and excluded from dominant society. Mr. Frivolous is thus caught in a quandary. Does he reveal his sexuality and thereby presume to reveal the truth about himself, or does he remain ambiguous and thereby risk collapsing sexual difference into a universalized, mythopoetic sexual experience? In addition, the absent gender identification of his playmate raises similar concerns.

Finally, it seems possible to answer these questions only with another: What difference does it make who is speaking? Why does it matter what sort of sexuality or gender Mr. Frivolous's affections are directed at? Could it not be supposed that such indifference is in fact because it no longer matters who is speaking? This position would seem attractive as an alternative to the rigidity of a system that demands identification. Indeed, it would suggest either the mythology of a pregendered, or "semiotic" (Kristeva), realm or a postgendered world, "liberated" from biology-as-destiny. Rather than celebrating the ambiguity of Mr. Frivolous's position as a liberative decision, however, it appears that the text uses this indifference precisely because it does *not* matter who is speaking, for, in any case, what he or she says always already returns him or her to the confines of a normative discourse. Mr. Frivolous will not, cannot, say anything different, cannot say anything at all that is not already within a processed sexuality. Indeed, he could very well be condemned by his name to saying nothing of importance. If the first two sections of the play demonstrate the limits of a hyperdiscourse and a hypersex as two poles of a sexual politic, both combine with the third to collapse that tension into a smothering sameness that condemns rather than celebrates what Foucault valorizes as "the stirring of an indifference" at the end of the author-function (Foucault 1977). Instead of freedom from authorial structures, sex is completely absorbed into sexuality. Instead of liberation, sex once again comports a hierarchic discourse, one from which, in this play, it was never free. To paraphrase Baudrillard's reading of *History of Sexuality:* when difference blends into indifference and indifference into difference, let's forget them both (1987, 49).

A Thought in Three Parts is a merciless rendition of the conversion of sex into institutional discourses that reveal, discuss, evaluate, and expound upon sexuality and that coterminously convert sex from pleasure to "truth." That Foucault renders sexuality as inescapably connected with discourse and power, and by extension with discipline, makes the entire argument obsolete for Baudrillard, for it collapses every term in the argument into a monolithic apparatus that is grounded on the possibility of the formation of societal relationships, laws, and ethics (what Baudrillard calls "the social"), which Foucault does not challenge: "The social itself must be considered a model of simulation and a form to be overthrown since it is a strategic form of value brutally positioned by capital and then idealized by critical thought" (Baudrillard 1987, 53). Rather than power producing resistance at every turn, power *seduces* because it collapses polarized meaning into its domain. Since power can no longer be held by a certain group, it is everywhere: for Foucault, a component of every relationship; for Baudrillard, nonexistent because ubiquitous. For Baudrillard, power is a simulation that is "executed according to a reversible cycle of seduction, challenge, and ruse (neither axis nor indefinite relay, but a cycle)" (43). In a sense, then, Foucault should be forgotten at the point he begins to speak of "indifference," for power is an illusion of perspectivist space, something that holds sway only when approached by classical thought. If this space is a simulation, overcoded by seduction, then power would seem to be only an internal constituent that makes no difference in any case.

Baudrillard exceeds his own argument here, however, for even if power is only a result of perspectivist space, the discourses that that space compels are still functional, still produce at least an illusory power that has an effect on the constitution of "bodies and sex." To jump to such a conclusion as Baudrillard's is to miss the route by which the text (Foucault's and Shawn's) terminates at "the ends of Man" (a notion that is always latent in Baudrillard) and is thus to miss the topography of the terrain. The "stirring of an indifference" might itself be caught in such a simulation, but the discursivity that produces—or, in Baudrillard's term, seduces—that indifference still suggests a certain ineluctability of discourse: even if "the social" is entirely simulated, it still has concrete effects on the body (e.g., the body can and will age and die). Yet, despite this reservation, Baudrillard's suspicion of Foucault's technology of sexuality should be kept in mind, because it suggests the nihilism inherent in power, a nihilism that cannot be easily overestimated.

While, in *A Thought in Three Parts*, no miraculous rebirth frees these characters from the "prison of the soul," from discourse in order that they might miraculously reveal themselves, the trajectory of the "thought" could also be read as a mapping of the consequences and shortcomings of certain received notions of sexuality. The first section would roughly correspond to Foucault's notion of how sex disappears through the mandate to talk about it, around it, and of its effects but never actually to experience pleasure as a direct result. The hyperdiscourse Sarah and David engage in reaches a point of pleasure only at the end, after they turn off the lights and the dialogue stops. They cannot talk directly about sex, but they construct an entire existence around it, on its discursive margins that, however designed to replicate sex, can only conceal it further as a disguised textual operation. These "other Victorians" (as Foucault terms contemporary society) are opposed by the four characters in "Youth Hostel" who perform their sexual acts with reckless abandonment, beyond the confines of any normative experience of sex. If, as a number of counterculture movements in the pre-AIDS era proposed, liberation would "come" through an exuberant proliferation of sexual acts, then these people, by the end of the section, should certainly have gained some space for themselves. Yet they seem worse off than David and Sarah, for they are all cold and alone, except for Judy, who is being beaten by Tom. This ending could be read two ways. Their isolation could be seen as the futility of hoping to supersede discourse through action, that to imagine the body as an unproblematic source or site for a liberative alternative is doomed to fail. Alternatively, the end could be read as the entry onto the scene of that very possibility, of the "inducement to talk about sex" that is the obverse side of the "repressive hypothesis." Yet to say that David and Sarah are better off because "at least they are talking" merely perpetuates a similar privileging of the discourse on/of sex over sex itself and, furthermore, is to assume the Victorianism of *Scientia Sexualis* that condemns sex to discourse in the first instance.

Perhaps a more interesting reading would be to say "yes, but . . . " to each possibility rehearsed above, for both have their attractions and their limitations. Constructing the body as an unproblematic site suggests a nostalgia for a mythical state that ignores the political operations that the body both produces and is subjected to, a state that apparently outshines any concrete possibility except its remythologization. The same thing can be said about the second reading, in only slightly different terms. To imagine that remaining silent about sexuality will erase its effects only perpetuates an optimism as nostalgic and unimaginable as to imagine that talking about it will remove it from discursive controls. Between these two readings would then have to be one that stresses the necessity of allowing for an ambiguous atmosphere, a reading that would value a detached fascination about sex and an indifference to its particulars. The third section, "Mr. Frivolous," seems to do just that. Yet the supposed indifference of this section also conflates gender and sexual preference in such a way that these confluences lose any real political consequence, a loss that would seem to eviscerate the very reasons for constructing an argument such as Foucault's.

In fact, this might also appear to be a point at which Foucault's own discourse on sexuality and power starts to unravel. Mr. Frivolous's inattention to his gender-specific companion could be read as a mystification of the process by which power relations in the sexual realm—and, by extension, the racial, classist, ageist realms—materialize ("the sexual realm is the political realm" [Acker 1984, 43]). Mr. Frivolous's silence on the identity of his partner betrays the fact that, despite his Baudrillardesque abandon in describing passion, it *does* matter who is speaking, for the same reasons that Foucault's own argument for the movement of indifference, especially in *The History of Sexuality*, is troubling. In fact, it could be argued that Foucault's recognition of the production by power of sexuality as an institutional discourse, as opposed to its existence as an attribute of the body, is crucial to understanding how sexuality produces its subjects in accordance with various discursive (i.e., institutional) needs. For example, Teresa de Lauretis points out that to construct sexuality as a social technology, as does Foucault, is useful precisely because it denaturalizes both the body as an ontological site and sexuality as a practice in favor of imagining such production and deployment as a phenomenon imbricated with the totalizing power of institutional discourses. At the same time, however, de Lauretis questions the valorization of "bodies and pleasure" in Foucault—"We must not think that by saying yes to sex, one says no to power. . . . The rallying point for the counterattack against the deployment of sexuality ought not then be sex-desire, but bodies and pleasure" (Foucault 1980a, 157)—for such "pleasure" is also a mystification of the sociopolitical position of sexuality: "For sexuality, not only in the general and traditional discourse but in Foucault's as well, is construed not as gendered (as having a male form and a female form) but simply as male" (de Lauretis 1987, 37). This blindness in sociosexual definitions of sexuality disregards how "even when it is located, as it very often is, *in* the woman's body, sexuality is an attribute or property of the male" (37). Consequently, without either attending to differentiation within the sexual between male and female, or problematizing how Western society (among others) constructs sexuality as predominantly male, any claim for "bodies and pleasure" will be limited, even as it does its best to unravel the technology of sexuality, by remaining blind to the coterminous production of a "technology of gender."

In a sense, the technology of gender, as de Lauretis configures it, represents a limit-text to any discourse on the body and sex. Mr. Frivolous's (and, by implication, Foucault's) silence on this technology reifies the dissemination of "Man" as a discursive regulator, for it suggests that the person he is not talking about, is forgetting, eliding, or losing as he apparently transgresses the discursive tradition that compels him to make that identification, is in the first and last analysis the *Same*, that is, male. This is not to say that male homosexuality cannot be and is not transgressive (as it certainly is in many instances). But, when Mr. Frivolous posits his sexuality as male-by-default, is this action really any different from the institutional actions that posit the violent elision of "that which is not male" as representing a "natural" order?

I would say that in fact Mr. Frivolous's action is, or could be, but only in as much as it can be thought through the trope of the ends of Man. Without this "end," it would be impossible to think "Otherwise," even though such a thought is, in the context of this play, no more than liminally present. To account for the damaging effects of a sexuality that is posited as always already male and, in accounting for it, to overcome it requires an erotics not available in the institutional apparatus in which and by which sexuality first appears. Transgression cannot appear within discourse. Indeed, it can only be accomplished through something else, some other possibility. As Maurice Blanchot puts it, "Transgression does not transgress the law, but carries the law away with it" (139). *A Thought in Three Parts* provides analogies to the historical processes that convert sex into sexuality, discourse into institution. Yet discourse, if it can in fact be imagined outside an institutional realm, still needs to be perverted, transgressed, exploded in order to disrupt its incarcerating operations as well as to avoid constructing the end of Man as simply an agentless pessimism that forebodes only more of the same or, on the other hand, disguises "Man's" reappearance in the guise of a promise of sexual liberation.

At this point, where Churchill's and Shawn's plays face the ineluctability of incarceration, at the threshold where discourse triumphs over pleasure, where knowledge cancels desire, Kathy Acker's *The Birth of the Poet* begins its delirious assault on the institutions and apparatus of sexuality and the State—begins, that is, "to carry away the law." In Acker's play, the institutional theater meets a recklessly calculated textuality that does away with the oppression and rigidity haunting contemporary social apparatus, that constructs desire in a form other than the narrative of lack, and that evokes, in the same (Artaudian) breath, the end of "Man." Here the end of Man raises the possibility of an *ars erotica* that is not attached to the utility of reproduction or the homogeneity (in Bataille's sense) of domination—or, for that matter, the possibility of affect and emotion. Yet it needs to be kept in mind that, while the invocation of an *ars erotica* suggests the pre-Christian societies of Greece and Rome that Foucault opposes to our own *Scientia Sexualis*, even those earlier structures embodied a normative desire (albeit constructed in fundamentally different terms) that undercut its own erotic possibilities through the erasure of difference.

Consequently, evoking "transgressive desire" as a liberative trope is fraught with its own problems, ones related to de Lauretis's critique of Foucault mentioned above. Simply put, the desire constructed in the context of *la pensé de dehor*, most notably in the writing of George Bataille and his followers, remains open to the charge that it is always already constructed in terms of a certain phallic economy, one that may problematize the law (of the father) but that remains almost entirely in that terrain. It is at this double-crossing of desire, this point at which desire seems almost ineluctably phallic, that Acker begins to write her own "history of the present," one that certainly does not follow any prescriptive literary or psychoanalytic maps.

In *The Birth of the Poet*, the illusion of character, the simple portrayal of a unified self, falls apart. Whereas in *Softcops* and *A Thought in Three Parts* the characters can be read as tropes for certain discursive operations, in *The Birth of the Poet* they remain at the limit of those operations, unable and, more significant, unwilling to account for an ontotheological state of being that resides within a particular discourse. The text itself makes indescribable its own theatricality; it continually defers the question of "authenticity" or "authority" until the point that these "master-tropes" of traditional textuality disappear. The terrorism in act 2, which drives Cynthia to suicide as she abandons Proprietus, leads finally to the appearance of the Other onstage. This Other, ostensibly in the form of Ali, evokes the event horizon of Western discourse, a horizon on which topographical features collapse into one another. The architectonics of *The Birth of the Poet* do not simply decompose the experience of desire into pain, nor do they vault desire into an aesthetic realm; instead, the play produces an affective realm configured according to emotions—a realm that is itself problematic for the official map of traditional logic-based thought, for it is not simply that thought's binary opposite: "If we can write histories of rationality, so too we can write histories of the emotions. It is necessary to underline the *s*, to call attention to the plural, so that we do not find ourselves only engaged in deconstructing the antinomy of reason and emotion, which is to say, making explicit what we already know" (Woodward 1990, 3). The appearance of emotions on an evacuated stage is significant, for emotions bespeak a language that at least offers the possibility for a world without domination, distrust, or disease.

The destructive force of desire is not only a diegetic event. Acker's text itself appropriates and cannibalizes several received notions of textuality. In this play, as well as in her novels, she liberally appropriates from the canonical literary tradition. The entire middle section of the play is taken almost verbatim from her *Great Expectations,* a novel about both living in the fallout of a suicided mother and a sexually and emotionally abusive father and the search for love in a world in which desire is a prison. Colette also appears. During Cynthia's last scene, when she refuses to accept her lot as the construct "woman," a refusal that causes her to stick razor blades in her arms and die in the streets surrounded by alcoholics, Colette and Renée profess their love in a scene that sardonically aestheticizes Cynthia's material conditions:

> "Tell me Renée. Are you happy?" . . . "Why, of course my dear Colette . . . . " "I didn't say I wanted it, I retorted." "I'm happy . . . but the sexual ecstasy is so great, I'm going to be physically sick." (316)

Acker's cannibalization of other people's literature is extensive; the title of the novel on which the play resides refers the reader back to another famous Western man who wrote novels, creating an expectation that Acker apparently has no compunction to fulfill. Her parasitical text resists its incorporation into the realm of truth, of universality, for it makes no pretension of having anything in common with the texts (in this case Dickens's) that obtain such status. By incorporating the section of dialogue from Colette's *The Pure and the Impure,* for example, Acker assembles a textuality that is itself a version of a collected (*not* collective) past that questions the ability of any one discourse, historical or literary, to account for all the threads of "the human race."

The Birth of the Poet is divided into three acts, which, like the sections in *A Thought in Three Parts,* cannot actually be considered acts because they are not really part of a coherent narrative. The first act lasts up until the stage explodes and the play ends: "Slowly the large window glass is cracking. After this cracking sound, all is totally still, suddenly BAM BAM BAM. Nuclear-solar leakage looks gray and red. The whole stage blows to bits and the play is over" (Acker 1986, 309).

The "World Workers" and coked capitalists seem mindless of the consequences of their actions other than to continually increase productivity as they try to meet production quotas in a perfect world in which nothing can fall behind schedule because everything is in perfect conformity with the logic of computers:

> *White World Worker 1*: The only thing we need to keep going is files. Files of the workers' medical insurance . . . life insurance . . . car insurance . . . theft insurance.
> *White WW 2*: This is the only reason we need workers. (307)

In the ever increasing speed of the late-capitalist universe, production is collapsed into circulation:

> *White WW 2*: Products are out-of-date. No one can afford to buy anyway. . . . We need workers who can understand what we're doing. Who will work harder because there is nothing to work for. (307)

In the Baudrillardian metastasis of pure circulation, the body and discourse are subsumed, and "movement becomes autonomous for survival" (309). The power of production, the economy of utility and reproduction, disappears in the feverish circulation of energy and power through the endlessly refined capitalist machinery until that circulation reaches its logical conclusion, that is, becomes uncontrollable. Power, in the instant before its disappearance, also becomes apparent.

> *Translucent Worker*: Power in its essence is in no way material, it has no essence at all in a philosophical sense, and it is an apparently unnameable figment of the imagination. (309)

Realizing the essential immateriality of power, however, cannot put the machines, or these workers, back on course; the energy they desperately produce is finally beyond categorization. Despite the well-oiled machines that produce multitudes of energy, the basic nucleic material is a force too powerful for those machines. While the workers and their masters have built a world that constantly produces more power, more force, more logic, more efficiency, it cannot contain leakage, nor can it stem atomic forces once they exceed a certain threshold. Late capitalism destroys the world along with its capital-induced frenzy in a crisis that is the mirror opposite of the energy crisis; instead of starvation, there is excess. After "the end of the world" (309), a brutal postapocalyptic scene surfaces.

In the second act, Cynthia and Propertius (who also appear in Acker's novel *Great Expectations*) discuss their sexual activities in a series of five sections. Cynthia appears to be the ideally submissive woman, completely enraptured about becoming Propertius' sex toy:

> *Cynthia:* Why aren't you grabbing my cunt every chance you get? I love fucking in public streets and why are you telling me you want to be friends and work with me more than you care about sex with me. (310)

For his part, Propertius, a Roman poet, is a hypermale who apparently uses Cynthia, and every other woman with whom he comes in contact, only for his own gratification:

> *Propertius:* If you read every poem in every anthology of Greek poetry, you wouldn't read one poem in which the character of the woman who's loved is described or matters. That's because women are goddamn sluts. They're goddamn sluts because the only thing they've got going for them are their cunts. (317)

Here and elsewhere, the text pillages Western literature, converting literary conventions into stark reminders of the terrorist grounds of canonical misogyny and aesthetics. By playing off prescriptive sexual stereotypes and pushing such representations beyond the point where it is possible to talk of "good" characters, the text makes a shambles of normative sexuality.

Cynthia's need for sex is not simply to be Propertius' plaything but also to articulate her desire in a manner other than the recounting of sexual adventures or conquests, without turning herself into an object:

> *Cynthia:* I think if you really worship sex, you don't fuck around. Danielle fucks around more than any of us and she's the one who doesn't care about sex.
> *Barbarella:* Most men don't like sex. They like being powerful and when you have good sex you lose all power.
> *Cynthia:* I need sex to stay alive. (313)

Why does Cynthia need sex to stay alive? Is it simply a desire to slip into the security and metastasis of the object position? Or is to "need sex"—which, according to Barbarella, is to "lose power"—to slip away from the discursivity of sex through a malignant neglect that has nothing to do with submission, except in its most ironic forms?[5] Is it to validate a certain "way of feeling, a different sensibility" (Deleuze 1982, 15), that is, to signify "histories of pity, resignation, sincerity, jealousy, tenderness, horror, and tranquility; of grief, abjection, disgust, boredom, fear, resentment, ecstasy, pride, bitterness, gratitude, and irritation" (Woodward 1990, 1), as a respite from the numbing sameness of incarcerating desire, which seems to be, despite enthusiastic denials, always reverting to normative categories of lack and loss? Is it an escape, that is, from normative antinomies? With Cynthia, the rules of sexuality are changed, the world of safe and normal discourse thrown out:

> No way to tell the difference between alive and dead. Criminalities which are understandable mix with religious practices, for people have to do anything to satisfy that which can no longer be satisfied we shall define sexuality as all that which can't be satisfied. (Acker 1986, 311)[6]

Cynthia's need to lose herself in sex could be accounted for as an attempt to escape the desolation of a conservative will to knowledge (one that equates knowledge with virtue), to escape the scrutiny of *Scientia Sexualis* through deliberately confronting her (erased) status.

In this case, Cynthia's desire is that which always already exceeds discourse, that which is unaccountable within normative sexuality and which, indeed, discourse must "discover" (as if within sexuality there were some great truth that would "satisfy people") in order to maintain the boundaries that create particular social arrangements. Indeed, when talking about Cynthia's abdication, the terrain opened up by Luce Irigaray for "the/a other woman," of a *jouissance* that speaks outside of the law of the father, that speaks an/other language, is an appropriate image.[7]

Yet her disenchantment with "power" is not simply a matter of appropriating forms of desire that pose one particular discursive position against another or reverse the law of the Same. When Cynthia speaks of her wish to "lose power," she also problematizes her position vis-à-vis desire as a normative category in that she does not remain passive, nor, however, does she reject her position outright. Cynthia—and, by implication, the entire play—moves in a space that would have to be situated between lack and desire, on neither side of binary polarity:

> *Cynthia:* I don't have any finesse I'm all over you like a raging blonde leopard and I want to go more raging. I want to go snarling and poisoning and teasing eek eek, curl around your hind leg pee, that twig over there. I want your specific piss shuddering out of your cock. I want you to help me. I need help. (310)

At the same time, the text never imagines Cynthia's condition in an idealist manner. Cynthia does not simply escape; the law, the father, the fallout from an apocalyptic culture still mark her world. She resides on the edge of an impossibility and thus must find, must constantly (re)invent, language at every turn.

The immediate physicality of Acker's graphic enunciations of desire contrasts sharply with the linguistic prescriptions of the two other plays considered here. In *Softcops*, the "small personal theatres" of discourse and power create a prison house for society, and, in *A Thought in Three Parts*, sex manifests only in sexuality, in desire's deferral to language. Indeed, in both plays, characters reside comfortably within their discursive systems, simply marking the operations of those positions. *The Birth of the Poet* articulates desire in two different figures, Cynthia and Propertius. Rather than a simple subject/object split, however, this bifurcation takes place on the subject side of the split. Both figures function as subjects, albeit in different ways, thereby calling into question the utility of a subject/object telos. By staging Cynthia alongside Propertius, two forms of desire are placed in proximity, forms that do not complement each other according to a normative scheme but, rather, that compete. Propertius' will to dominate is matched by Cynthia's will to escape domination, to create her own agency. The desperation of Cynthia's condition (one that, it should be remembered, is not that of an actual character but of a discursive position) derives from her inability to find a place in a world made to order for Propertius:

> *Cynthia:* Why can't you ever once do something that's not allowable? I mean goddamnit. Hit me. Do anything. Do something. (313)

Of course, "doing something" is exactly what cannot be done. Cynthia can beg to be beaten, but, in the confines of Propertius' discourses, "On the Nature of Art," hers is a desire that can never be born. By needing aesthetics in order to create, Propertius must remove himself from the physical, concrete surface of desire that Cynthia inhabits. His will to freeze objects as monuments to his sexual and artistic conquests also freezes desire into a subject/object relationship, a relationship out of which Cynthia can never speak. Propertius the poet, the institutional receptacle of value, can, however, be born on the breakdown of Cynthia's autonomy, or perhaps, more perniciously, be born to cause Cynthia's breakdown. Cynthia, it could be said, once again disappears along with her desire.

In the realm of the textual, however, it appears that something else occurs. Cynthia is not used simply to posit either woman-as-object of desire or woman-as-desiring subject, that is, is not coerced into remaining within a system that can only bespeak desire as need for something/someone else (read object). The text's refusal to give her a discursive position and, conversely, its refusal to construct her as the passionate, passive Other of Western discourse is hardly because of any hesitation over destroying the bonds of articulate discourse. Rather, it can be read as an attempt to articulate the discursive margins of the stage, a place in which desire is in constant danger of exceeding itself and thus becoming totalitarian (as in the capitalist universe of the first act) and in which the consequences, for both Cynthia and Propertius, of failing to articulate that desire is to fall back into silence (for Cynthia) and fascism (for Propertius). Indicative of this articulation is that, when Cynthia does slice her arms in the alcoholic streets, her death is preempted by a scene from *The Pure and the Impure*. Rather than a death scene, a large section of Colette's novel is lifted verbatim, without any acknowledgment of the source, and pasted over Cynthia's dying image. While certainly the purloined page can be made to make sense as a recording of the lives of upper-class women living on the edge of a morally stagnant society, its juxtaposition to a dying Cynthia makes it, if anything, a horrendous rendition of the failure of early twentieth-century modernism to provide a space for its late twentieth-century equivalent. When taken in the further context of the "great expectations" that act 2 invokes (an act borrowed almost entirely from Acker's novel *Great Expectations*), Renée's statement that "the sexual ecstasy is so great, I'm going to be physically sick" (316) becomes ironic. Because of the sudden and inexplicable appearance of the Colette passage, there is a suspicion throughout the act that, as Judith Butler might say, Cynthia is simply and consciously playing a role: "In what senses, then, is gender an act?. . . Although there are individual bodies that enact [cultural meanings] by becoming stylized into gendered modes, this 'action' is a public action" (140). Butler's suspicion of the "authenticity" of a position like Cynthia's casts doubt on Cynthia's categorization as victim and, in fact, questions the epistemological grounds of her relationship to Propertius in a manner similar to the indeterminacy posed by the nuclear leakage of the first act.

The final two sections of act 2 are discussions "On the Nature of Art" and "Conversations To People Who Aren't Here." Both feature Propertius' sadistic rants on the acts and quality of *his* desire:

> *Propertius:* The worst thing about women is all these emotions. Take the hole I slept with last night. Sure she moaned hard when I stuck my dick in her. But did she have any idea that I didn't feel? (317)

and his sublimation of that aggression into a life for art:

> *Propertius:* Sure I'm a macho pig. Why should I pretend. . . . Everything but art is a second-class existence. (317)

Propertius seems to want nothing more than to rechannel his sexual desire into art, to avoid the humiliating desperation of Cynthia's madness, yet it is not simply a matter of constructing Cynthia as mad and then trying to "cure" her. Cynthia's "madness" (which could be read as affect) threatens the law, threatens the subject/object relationship, and consequently is constantly on the verge of disappearance:

> *Propertius:* I don't want you, slut, because desire is mad and I don't want to be mad. (319)

Propertius' desire to avoid madness is the inverse of Cynthia's desire to lose herself. In the section "Conversations To People Who Aren't Here," Propertius carries on an extended monologue with Cynthia as its object. It reveals a need for control so desperate that it borders on the hysterical:

> *Propertius:* Looking everywhere looking everywhere looking everywhere looking everywhere: each human is so stupid it's a ravenous wolf. Long red pointed fingernails will separate the cunt lip flesh, then dig into the soft purple, and around the protrusion

of the nipple right there, another fingernail. This is why you can't run away from me. There's only obsession. Love will turn on the lover and gnaw. (319)

Stuck between wanting Cynthia in order to escape his obsession with control and need (in the psychoanalytic sense) and refusing to give into the love that gnaws and tears, Propertius extends himself across a landscape that allows him virtually nothing in terms of his emotions. This landscape is defined by Augustus:

> *Augustus:* Artists who are men have to change the world. When they start paying attention to emotions, what are emotions? they're helping the power hawks destroy the social bonds people need to live. (317)

One element of the landscape is his need to be a "macho pig" (in his own words): his friend Augustus and his attitude toward women are examples of this. The other element is his understanding of Cynthia's desperation, the desperation of emotion in the face of a world order that constructs desire as an apparatus of control (i.e., patriarchy).

> *Cynthia:* Madness makes an alcoholic sober, keeps the most raging beast in an invisibly locked cage, turns seething masses of smoke air calm white, takes a junky off junk as if he's having a pleasant dream. . . . I am only an obsession. . . . Watch out. Madness is a reality, not a perversion. (316)

For Propertius, following Cynthia into the reality of madness in this instance is a voyage into an unmarked topology that involves giving up the privileges of patriarchy. For Cynthia, these privileges are something she never had: she explores madness as a relief from patriarchy. For Propertius, confronting that stepping-off point, letting go of the structures and benefits of his social position, involves alienation from the power nexus of the literary establishment (which is a synecdoche for an entire social hierarchy).

Augustus: (Through the lips of his literary counselor Maecenas.) You're not a poet and you're not a real man because you write about emotion. Men are people who take care of the world, who care that people get enough to eat, who stop the greedy hawks at least from seizing more power and underhanded control. . . .

Propertius: One day, Maecenas, you're going to realize you're not rational and then, suddenly ignorant and desperate, you'll leave your politics and run to me. (317)

Despite his recognition of the limits of his social position, of that position's inability to account for irrationality, or for Cynthia's desire, Propertius finally does not give up that position. It is interesting, too, that Propertius does not go mad but, instead, becomes a poet, for it suggests that the problems both figures run into in losing control are structural, endemic to the system and machinations that form their world.

Propertius: (To Cynthia who isn't in front of him.) I know you've been going through hell because I've been refusing to speak to you. I know the moment I stopped talking to you, you slit your wrist (you did that just cause when you were in your teens you regularly cut your arms with a razor blade to show yourself you were horror), then more seriously you got an ovarian infection because your ovaries had been rejected. You tried, I know you tried you did avoid me (except when you phoned ten times a day). (318)

When Propertius abandons his posturing, he discovers the literal madness of the world Cynthia inhabits. Her pain becomes an entreaty to her world, an offer for understanding. Yet the pain is not something Propertius can share, and thus he is born a poet, constantly sublimating his emotions away from the madness of losing control, into the "objectness" of art as artifact and into the channels of patriarchy that constitute in the first instance the subject/object relationship. "Cynthia" (read woman) represents to Propertius desire constructed as outside of discursivity, as the subjectivity imagined by Teresa de Lauretis as both inside and outside ideology, as a "literal madness" that threatens to explode his world with the same violence and transgression as the runaway atoms and nuclear leakage that do away with the capitalist world in the first act. The final section of act 2, "Conversations To People Who Aren't Here," shows Propertius on his knees in front of an absent (suicided) Cynthia, desperately trying to explain to her why he can't lose control, why he must reject her as an equal in order to maintain himself.

The consequences of his rejection are stupendous—as devastating to the discursive position he inhabits as the explosions are to the capitalist world at the end of the first act:

> *Propertius:* Cynthia walked away from me, and I woke up. *(To Cynthia who isn't in front of him.)* I don't want you, slut, because desire is mad and I don't want to be mad. (319)

His rejection, which are the last lines of the act, reveals the inarticulateness of his position at its most vulnerable moment and the moment in which it could begin to account for the Other. Instead, Propertius abandons Cynthia for the safety of patriarchy's silence. In the face of this inability to say anything, that is, in the terms Western society constructed around the possibility and telos of total knowledge about the self (a knowledge that cannot, by definition, encompass madness), the second act mirrors the desolation of the physical landscape of the first act. In the silences of its incoherent stutterings emerges a force that speaks in a manner that the "West" can conceive of only as silence. As the simplistic normativizing categories such as "gender" and "desire" erode, or unwind, Propertius' act of rejection appears as a final doomed try at maintaining the authority those categories provided.

The final act, written in Arabic with both Roman transliterations and English translations, records Ali's singular adventures in a bazaar, a mosque, and with a witch. The strangeness of the language, especially when compared to the previous two acts, foregrounds a substantial shift in perspective. Unlike the vivid interiors of capitalist overproduction or the breakdown of liberative desire into fascism, act 3 begins where the inarticulateness that supposedly marks "the end of the world" lets off. The first stage direction reads: "At first there is only language and nothing else" (320). Except for the letter that Ali writes to his "mommy," the entire act is a third-person narration of his actions. Whereas in act 2 it is sometimes unclear who is speaking, no one speaks in this act, except in the letter. Ali's adventures do not explain anything. The short, descriptive sentences simply portray actions taken without any effort to understand or consider why anything happens. Other than disguising himself as the man who shot Ronald Reagan, "Ali Warnock Hinkley," he travels without the historical baggage that haunts the other (Western) characters. The episode with his mommy, in which he writes her a letter on "the day of Reagan's attempted assassination," suggests that a violence invades his world similar to that which was present in the second act: "Dear Mom, Your guts stink. I hate your hair. . . . We are going to have to kill each other because there is no other way out of this relationship. . . . Are we supposed to have sex, mom, even though you're dead?" (326). Ali's letter functions as a response against the subjectivity that enslaves Propertius and Cynthia, that wants to understand his world, that wants to penetrate it to discover his motivations, turn him into an object of surveillance of the "human sciences." Yet the obliqueness of his actions refuses surveillance. The language in which his actions are recorded is constructed as an event in itself; its concreteness is opposed to the insubstantiality of confessions that reveal the truth indirectly. Here is an *ars erotica* that is unknowable, that exists in language, that frustrates the humanist scene not through an explosive outpouring of sexuality, as in the second act of *A Thought in Three Parts*, but through a refusal to talk directly, a renunciation of the concept of confession, which has made of bodies and pleasure a discursive prison.

When Ali appears onstage, Acker and Fassbinder intersect, if only for a moment. In Fassbinder's film *Angst Essen Die Seele* (translated as *Ali: Fear Eats the Soul*), the character named Ali, an autoworker in a German city, plays a similar role to Acker's Ali in that he occupies a position outside of the narrative that happens around him, not as an observer but not actually as a participant either. The film is about

Ali in almost an ancilliary manner, as if he only need exist as a mute figure for the film to take place. Fassbinder's Ali meets and marries an elderly German woman, who shares with him the daily ostracism that Ali faces as a foreign worker. Unlike Acker's Ali, however, Fassbinder's Ali is completely confined within the bourgeois German culture, even though it never accepts him. His existence is necessary to the function of the capitalist state, yet socially unacceptable. Finally, Fassbinder's Ali bears the weight of society's rejection. In the film's penultimate scene, he collapses from a perforated stomach lining, and, in the last scene, he lies in a hospital as a German doctor describes his ulcer as a typical malady of foreign workers, an incurable, recurring condition brought on by the stress of low-wage labor and hostile working conditions. In *Angst Essen Die Seele*, Ali is silenced by his society, and thus his body begins to eat him.

In *The Birth of the Poet*, Ali's particular kind of silence is incomprehensible to the confessional mode of Western psychological thought; his condition as Other corrodes that thought, acts on it like an ulcer that, in inhabiting hitherto silenced spaces, exposes its inadequacies as a universal model. Both Fassbinder and Acker complicate the normal associations of textual and narrative progressions—Fassbinder by discarding any notion of plurality and acceptance, Acker by emphasizing what "progress" cannot contain. Yet it is also at the point of the appearance of the Other that their paths part. When Acker's Ali takes over act 3, he manages to reinvest the play with a sense of the consequences of the Other, of the enemy that stands outside of the discursive tradition that Propertius and Cynthia act out. He is an Other with agency, with the ability to say and not say what humanism does not and cannot hear: that all men are not created equal, nor do they all hold the same truths to be self-evident, but, instead, "truth," "man," and "equality" are discursive agents of a power/knowledge configuration that defines a particular historical *episteme*.

The illusion of humanism is that meaning is apparent, that it is available to any and all of its participants. Furthermore, on this stage, knowledge proceeds forthwith to investigate and understand (read, after Foucault, discipline and punish). Yet, in the final act of this play, the well-lighted economies of humanism are strangely absent; it is as if a map with no coordinates, or rather a map whose coordinates are deliberately misconstrued, appears. Ali appears in a bazaar, talks to a witch, disguises himself as a regicide (Ali Warnock Hinkley), and speaks in a language that moves from right to left on the page. His narrated actions foreground a difference that is, at every turn, fundamentally outside the Western tradition of reason and rationality. Indeed, it is worthwhile to recollect at this point one of the final stage directions of act 1: "The whole stage blows to bits and the play is over" (309). For the play to be over before the first act even ends signals an unusual occurrence, one whose full significance does not become apparent until act 3. Ali's role in this act is narrated, but it is a narration without any identifiable location, without an omniscient presence behind grounding the story in a metaphysical framework. The position of the narrator is called into question, if not rejected outright, in this act, because all it can do is describe acts and record utterances without either commenting on or giving context for what is done or said:

There is no centralization. There are no thoughts. There are no goals. There aren't expectations. (328)

These lines, unattributed statements, give rise to the suspicion that there is no logic in the act other than that of anarchy, that the inability of the narrator to give any logical context to Ali's "story" is somehow the consequence of an encounter with the Other, one that does not result in simple colonialization or subjugation. The result of this encounter is the apparent randomized incidences that Ali experiences, incidences that signal the dissolution of narrative certainty because they add up to no coherent whole.

Further support for the idea that the discourses designed to "know thyself" are silenced when confronted with the Other lies in the constant unidentified shifts in character and the three linguistic systems present on the page:

'Ali goft
Ali said

Inja sagi hast.
Here is a dog.

Inga gorbe' hast.
Here is a cat.

Inja zendegi nist.
Here there is no life.

Hic ciz ra namikoni
You don't do anything.

Tanbal i.
You're lazy.

Be hic cuz 'aqide daram.
I don't believe anything.

Dar jahanye 'aquidegan namiziam.
I don't live in a world of beliefs.

Bashari az jahan hic ciz ra kay yaft?
When has a human gotten anything from the world?

Shah o pedar ra nadaram v az hame kas nefrat daram va man xelafe xod
    mijangam.
I have no king no father I hate everyone and I'm in continuous war against
    the self.

Har ciz ra miguyam: hickas dar har surat in zaban ra nadanad.
I say anything no one knows this language anyway.

Jense mo'annasam beto baz ast.
My vagina is open to you.

(330–31)[8]

The shifts in script (Arabic to Roman to English) are matched by shifts
in speaker (narrator to Ali to an unidentified woman). These changes
are not signaled in any way and thus hopelessly complicate any attempt to identify who might be speaking at any given moment. The
"continuous war against the self" that Ali wages reflects this confu-

sion, for, in doing so, Ali refuses any specific location that could thus be subjected to the various discourses that have arisen to deal with the self. Furthermore, Ali's avoidance of these discourses suggests that to transgress, to escape the prisons of the soul that characters in the other plays of this chapter inhabit, means also the disappearance of the sign of "Man."

The Birth of the Poet follows an arc that incessantly problematizes its own conditions. The text sacrifices the illusion of desire—the sequences of a well-made play in which desire is happily played out as a desire for something or someone—as a "superobjective" and, instead, brings desire itself onto the stage as a weapon against aesthetic sterility. Yet Acker's play refuses inscription into the idealist tradition of "evolutionary" change within the context of the drama. It shows the body as a site of contestation and destruction that is intimately bound to its own repression. Desire, as staged here, goes farther than, for example, Phoebe Zeitgeist's countererotics, which relentlessly replaces one fascism (the State) with another (anarchy). In *The Birth of the Poet*, desire destroys the "mommy-daddy-me" mentality of the "Holy Family" (Deleuze and Guattari) by overcoding its institutionality with the screams of its victims:

> *Cynthia:* Just why are you fucking me? You've got a girlfriend named Trick and you love her. . . . DON'T FUCK ME CAUSE YOU LIKE MY WORK. (311)

That desire can obtain not as a desire for the "truth" (the father, the mother, the self) but, rather, as a descent into a purely visceral experience wherein normative behavior loses control (goes mad, as it were) evokes the possibility that universality, as promised by power/knowledge systems, is itself only a contingency and, in its extreme form, yet another form of fascism. The "simultaneous contrasts, extravagances, incoherences, half-formed misshapen thoughts, lousy spellings" (311) that inhabit the second act leave the characters scrambling to create space in the play for themselves, despite the fact that, by the end, any notion of "self" is impossible. The third act is no longer "about" anything in the sense that it cannot, will not, reveal any more truths about its objects. The final two characters onstage, Ali and a witch, are both conspicuously absent from the "official" map of Western humanism. Ali, the inscrutable Other of Fortress Europa (the dominion of the concrete universal), a figure in black to be crusaded against, buried in the desert storms of Western fascism, and the witch, for centuries persecuted in the most violent manner by the State, invade the privileged position of the stage's last word but relentlessly refuse participation in its cathartic desire for closure.[9] Ali never attempts to transcend either the body or his physical condition; the "Man" who would want some "truth" to materialize at this point is left to watch Ali's impassive actions bear witness to a pain so indescribable that it causes the "Man" to falter (and, when Ali disguises himself as an antioedipalized Ali Warnock Hinkley, this threat is only continued). It is the pain of silence, of the silenced, of an inarticulateness that has no ground on which to stand, that finally speaks. The previous two acts have undermined the aesthetic monuments of progress and universality on which humanism stands; the final act presents *nothing* in the sense that Ali's actions are inscrutable, that they belong to other worlds uninhabitable by Man, that they are unreadable within that domain. Finally, rather than wallowing in ontology, these characters leave, and the stage "is left with the cries of peacocks" (334). Even the invocation of "pain," of a cathartic justification for action, is transformed by the cries of the peacocks into yet another silent monument at the end of history.

Where the characters of *Softcops* and *A Thought in Three Parts* find themselves further enmeshed in normative behavior and social apparatus, Ali forces the stage to acknowledge its limitations. Quite simply, there is not a discursive tradition in which to contain him that is without recourse to the insane sexual violence that Propertius and his band of "poets" represents. In the world in which capitalism has failed through its own logic, in which, in the aftermath of that collapse, language is impelled to explore the unseemly, dirty contours of its effects on living bodies, there is nothing to be said. Not because everything is (always) already said in the structure, in the discursivity of structure, but, rather, because that structure is confronted with an event that leaves it as inarticulate as Phoebe Zeitgeist's victims at the end of *Blood on the Cat's Neck*. Ali does not need to masquerade as a murderous father, however; he needs simply to abandon the discursive tradition in order for it to no longer be able to include him, that is, to betray its own failure as a universal.

The Birth of the Poet is a limit-text on which the excesses of humanism and traditional representation flounder. Between the graphic violence of Propertius and Cynthia's world and Ali's journey through a forbidden night of unspeakable desires, the notion of Man can only acknowledge the fundamental repressions (here in the form of misogyny) that it evokes and, in doing so, admit that it has no way of accounting for Ali's experiences except through expelling, in an all too violent manner, the occupants of his world. The immediacy of Acker's play, its appropriation of literary conventions and cultural tropes on its way to the end of humanism, suggests that the seeds of discontent are built into the humanist model, that in attempting to contain all possibilities it manages to repress in a fascistic manner what it cannot readily contain, and that only through failure can humanism continue. *The Birth of the Poet* utilizes irony and parody as an alternative to despair, but the laughter heard in Cynthia's voice or in Ali's footsteps does not in itself provide anything like a happy ending. Rather, it suggests that still another stage is needed, one that can have everything, and then again nothing, to do with "the Man." The point that Edward Said makes at the end of *Orientalism*, that a simple reversal of perspectives on the "Orient" is not enough, that an entirely different perspective needs to emerge, should be well noted in the theater:

The answer to Orientalism is not Occidentalism. No former "Oriental" will be comforted by the thought that having been an Oriental himself he is likely—too likely—to study new "Orientals"—or "Occidentals"—of his own making. If the knowledge of Orientalism has any meaning, it is in being a reminder of the seductive degradation of knowledge, of any knowledge, anywhere, at any time. Now perhaps more than before. (328)

At the end of humanism is not the end of the world. Certainly, the various apparatus, incarceral mechanisms, and power grids created in and over the sociopolitical field of this *epistème* might suggest that all that is possible are the incessant endgames of a humanist ahistoricism; certainly, Churchill's and Shawn's plays map this terrain. But, at the edges of this thought, at the very point at which this thought, any thought, recedes, it indeed seems as if Other sensibilities, marked and coded in ways unimagined in the humanist scene, begin to appear. Maybe it is on this edge that the poet is born, even if, in this case, the "poet" is something indiscernibly abstract, a mere ghost of his or her institutional form.

"The Fractured I ≠ the Dissolved Self": Ethnic Identity in Frank Chin and Cherríe Moraga

Something must be said. Must be said that has not been *and* has been said
before. . . . It will take a long time for living cannot be told, not merely told:
living is not livable. Understanding, however, is creating, and living, such an
immense gift that thousands of people benefit from each past or present life
being lived.
　　　　　　　　　　　—Trinh T. Minh-ha, *Woman, Native, Other*

Only a black person alienated from black language-use could fail to understand
that we have been deconstructing white people's languages and discourses since
that dreadful day in 1619 when we were marched off the boat in Virginia.
Jacques Derrida did not invent deconstruction; *we* did!
　　　　　　　　　　　—Henry Louis Gates, Jr., *The Future of Literary Criticism*

At the end of humanism is not the end of the world. Contemporary
ethnic-identified writers, among others, have pushed the notion of
the Other that appears in post-structuralism well beyond what is
possible in that body of theory. While not all ethnic-identified writers
consciously use post-structuralist, or any, theory, much ethnic-identified writing contains critiques of authority, authorship, teleology,
and narrative that coincide with concerns similar to those in the theory I have used so far in this project. In order to explore certain of the
potential theorizations of the Other that are inherent in post-structuralist thought, I want to read two dramatic texts written by ethnic-
identified writers. These include *The Chickencoop Chinaman* by Frank
Chin and Cherríe Moraga's *Giving Up the Ghost*. These texts draw
attention to the construction in Western thought of the Other's relationship to a normativized, normal Same to which the Other is infe-
rior. Furthermore, despite their apparently traditional forms, certain
aspects of these ethnic-identified texts are uncontainable within a
theoretical master-narrative.[1] Through this reading, I hope some of
the philosophical and political implications of a heterogeneous stage

space that have emerged in the previous chapters will also be followed up on and expanded in terms of a multicultural world.

Chin's and Moraga's texts represent different points of view on the struggles of an ethnic group to form an identity—and to lose an identity; the former is to gain a sense of self-definition, and the latter is to escape the hegemony of dominant culture.

> The constituency of "the ethnic" occupies quite literally a "pre-post"-erous space where it has to actualize, enfranchize, and empower its own "identity" and coextensively engage in the deconstruction of the very logic of "identity" and its binary and exclusionary politics. Failure to achieve this doubleness can only result in the formation of ethnicity as yet another "identical" and hegemonic structure. (Radhakrishnan 199)

The "doubleness" that Radhakrishnan identifies as an underlying question of ethnic identity is central to the plays I consider here. By grouping them together, I hope to approach the question of difference first addressed in chapter 1 from the perspective of the particular works and the questions of ethnicity they evoke, rather than, as in the other chapters, from a theoretical model. This approach will begin to dissolve (albeit problematically) the narrative through-line of my project as well as to speak in a language that is not necessarily recognized by, but at the same time by no means excluded from, the theoretical language used so far.

Yet the approach isn't the same as doing sociology, anthropology, or demographic analysis. A central challenge for theory and theater today is to find ways in which to speak that take into account the consequences of a coalition of culturally defined voices, that don't assume that "class struggle" or some other transcendental signifier can structure every effective resistance or access to power, and that aren't afraid to risk the potential "powerlessness" of a position that, in its multiplicity and openness, can be drowned or lost. The consequences of "losing identity" while retaining a voice as a member of the traditional hegemonic elite (which is, when institutional affiliations are weighed, the position of the theorist) is a crucial element of post-structuralist theory that has only rarely been fully acknowledged. While in one sense positioning the address of this chapter so that it remains within the structures of a particular theoretical arena again excludes the "Others" that I presume to write about, and apparently avoids relinquishing the privilege of a certain sociohistorical position, in another sense it is the only address that I can maintain, for, in the process of "speaking with" or listening to ethnic and postcolonial voices, I am still a historically and politically constituted "subject" and, as such, cannot simply assume an "Other" voice with which to speak or pretend that, as if by magic, I can "suspend" the question of my own positionality.

Two complications arise at this point. The first is that, while my construction of the Other as everything that is not included in the realm of traditional theoretical discourse is indeed problematic, I want to emphasize that I do so only tentatively. While certainly raising the voice of the Other as constructed within Platonism is strategically important in the context of traditional Western metaphysics, this construction is less useful elsewhere, for it is still beholden to a "margin-center" universe that evokes certain racist overtones, at least when used uncritically. In fact, the whole process of naming, in the sense of providing certainty, should be viewed with suspicion, at least in the context of a post-structured theater.

> To speak . . . unproblematically of a single Black, Feminist, or Third World model of revolution is as repressive as it is naive. These emergences are pressing for a different language, a different politics and temporality, for an infinitely complex program of action that has to fulfill the following objectives: empowerment and enfranchisement of contingent "identities," the overthrow of the general hegemony of Identity, and the prevention of the essentialization/hypostasis and the fetishization of "difference." (Radhakrishnan 210)

Whatever remarks made here that tend toward creating definitions of ethnicity are only a part of an attempt to negotiate some of the contradictions inherent in any subject position.

The second point that needs to be addressed before continuing is the gesture made in the title of this chapter toward Johann Gottlieb Fichte's historically preemptive rejection of the powerlessness of the traditional subject position after deconstruction: "the fractured 'I' does not equal the dissolved self." What is intimated here is crucial to this project as a whole, and to theory's current juncture. Post-structuralist theory has been accused of abandoning the subject at exactly the moment in which those groups historically denied subjectivity are able to access it. It is true that post-structuralist theory claims that the subject is not unified since there is no foundational or transcendental cogito impelling that position, and, furthermore, what subjectivity does appear does so as an effect of ideology. This is not to say that the subject position accrues no authority or has no access to power in its concrete functions or that the illusion of subjectivity maintained by ideological apparatus does not have actual, material consequences but, rather, that this position is always contestable. The problem comes when theory refuses or "forgets" to consider the investments of a fragmented subjectivity, of a position that is open and multiple, of a position that has the potential to interface with a plurality of identities. To slip between various locations on the cultural map need have nothing to do with quietude or despair. Rather, such slipperiness is clearly advantageous as a survival strategy, since it can elude the colonizing elements of the stage.

Until very recently, Chinese American playwrights have found only sporadic recognition in mainstream theater, with David Henry Hwang as one notable exception to this rule.[2] Hwang has produced work on Broadway and the major regional repertory theaters and thus is considered a "serious" playwright. Because of these successes, he is also dutifully recorded in publications such as *American Theatre* and other institutions. Although Hwang's work forms a critique of racist society, the forms in which he works are evidently acceptable enough to the dominant theater community to be produced as large-scale enterprises. Furthermore, Hwang, the most widely known Chinese American playwright, does not actually construct a positive identification for his characters. As James Moy argues in "David Henry Hwang's *M. Butterfly* and Philip Kan Gotanda's *Yankee Dawg You Die:* Repositioning Chinese-American Marginality on the American Stage," self- and cultural identity are two central issues in Chinese American theater:

> The popular acceptance of *these* disfigured Chinese characters despite their Asian-American authorship does not signify an assimilation of the Chinese or Asianness into the American Mainstream, but rather a mere repositioning of their marginality, and the creation of new "play" figures for the West. (314)[3]

Yet, even with Hwang's widespread acceptance in the theater mainstream, and other playwrights in somewhat less well-known circles, there hardly has been a universal acceptance of Asian American theater. The 1990 New York production of *Miss Saigon* is a reminder of the lack of insight so often evinced in mainstream theater toward Asian Americans and others. When the producers of *Miss Saigon* wanted to open a New York run, they decided to cast Jonathan Pryce, a Caucasian, in the role of the "Eurasian" pimp. The decision was immediately challenged by the Actors Equity Association and by Asian American groups that felt that an Asian American should be cast. By refusing to do so, the producers effectively erased the possibility that cultural differences might effect any substantive difference onstage. That Pryce may or may not have been the best actor is in a sense not the question, for it assumes that the issue of representation is one that exists in a void and is without any actual, material consequence. In playing the Eurasian character, Pryce displaced, once again, an Asian American actor at a time when many Asian Americans are struggling for recognition in major roles. Daryl Chin summarizes certain of the complexities in this issue by stating that "interculturalism hinges on the questions of autonomy and empowerment. To deploy elements from the symbol system of another culture is a very delicate enterprise. In its crudest terms, the question is: when does that usage act as cultural imperialism?" (174). Given the history of Asian Americans in this country, such neglect of the political and economic conditions of Asian American theater workers can all too easily be read as another example of imperialism.

In *The Chickencoop Chinaman*, Frank Chin must create a location and a politics of identity amid a world that both shatters his identity and tries to provide instead a ready-made "Chinese American" character. Unable to pass as European American (and therefore not "American"), several generations removed from his ancestral homeland (historically, many Asian Americans emigrated to North America, and especially California, many generations earlier than most Europeans), and overwhelmed by the sense that he is not accepted by either community, the protagonist, Tam Lum, struggles with the split between "Asian" and "American." Tam, a Californian, is in Pittsburgh to interview Charlie Popcorn, the one-time trainer and supposed father of Tam's childhood boxing hero, Ovaltine Jack Dancer. Although Tam is seemingly on a quest for the Ideal Father, for a male figure to provide him with a "true" identity, he continually subverts the patriarchal structures he encounters and problematizes to absurdity paternity per se. His inability to accept the fathers he finds, or who are forced upon him, raises questions about his position vis-à-vis the dominant State apparatus that constructs him as part of a minority, and therefore secondary, discourse. By refusing to assimilate like the writer Tom and realistically doubtful about his ability, as a fourth-generation Californian, to be a true Chinese, Tam traverses a never-never land of cultural icons such as the Lone Ranger, Helen Keller, and the Hong Kong Dream Girl. He searches for his "roots," as it were, but knows full well that "Chinamen are made, not born" (Frank Chin 6), that his identity, rather than remaining fixed to a national heritage—of China, of the United States, of Europe—is a composite of "junk-import lies, railroad scrap iron, dirty jokes, broken bottles, cigar smoke, Cosquilla Indian blood, wino spit, and lots of milk of amnesia" (6).

The Chickencoop Chinaman focuses on the question of identity and of forming a sense of identity that is not inherited without reflection from a culture that had no use for Chinese people except as indentured servants, day laborers, and laundry workers. The problem of identity for Chinese Americans exists not only in the play but in the world as well. Elaine Kim argues that the very notion of an Asian American identity is to a certain extent a creation foisted upon people of Asian descent by U.S. society: "Asian America is after all itself a creation of white racism that groups nationalities and activities together, making it possible to blame—and murder—a Chinese American out of frustration over competition from Japanese auto manufacturers" (Kim 1987, 89). In her essay "Defining Asian American Realities through Literature," Kim demonstrates the difficulties of creating an identity based on a notion of a fixed "I" or transcendental notion of self for many Chinese American writers (and, indeed, for others outside the mainstream of cultural identity in this country). Since the United States' dominant culture has never accepted Chinese as "Americans," and because the dominant racial paradigm in the United States is still northern European, the Chinese remain in a cultural "ghetto":

> So much writing by Asian Americans is focused on the theme of claiming an American, as opposed to Asian, identity that we may begin to wonder if this constitutes accommodation, a collective colonized spirit—the fervent wish to "hide our ancestry," which is impossible for us anyway, to relinquish our marginality, and to lose ourselves in an intense identification with the hegemonic culture. Or is it in fact a celebration of our marginality and a profound expression of protest against being defined by domination? (Kim 1987, 88)

Chinese American literature has reflected this split personality to a degree, with the majority of writers looking for some resolution between the two terms, and two identities. Amy Ling attempts to avoid the problems associated with the split identity of the term *Chinese American* in her term *Chinamerican* and embraces as part of a cultural literature both work that plays up dominant stereotypes and work that rejects those stereotypes: "In removing the hyphen, I wish to assert that we're not a wobbly balancing act but something together, a solid wholeness" (1981, 77).

Other writers, however, have seen this unification project as inherently misleading and ultimately damaging. Frank Chin is adamant that what has been perceived as Chinese America's dual cultural status, both Chinese and American, is a fabrication. Disassociated from Chinese culture and heritage because of both physical proximity and the legacy of intolerant immigration controls that forbade Chinese men and women to marry and kept Chinese women out of the United States, the Chinese heritage of "jade and oolong tea," of a mystic reserve, is a myth that bears no relation to Chinese America's contemporary situation: "We have been encouraged to believe that we have no cultural integrity as Chinese-Americans" (Frank Chin, Chan, and Wong 197). Jeffery Paul Chan, Shawn Wong, and Frank Chin have made an effort to question commonly perceived notions of Chinese Americans and to show how the literary distortions of mainstream culture have created a false image of their culture: "The myth of being either/or and the equally goofy concept of the dual personality haunted our lobes while our rejection by both Asia and white America proved we were neither one nor the other" (197). Accordingly, the Chinese American is perpetually in a state that is neither American or Chinese, and, as the editors of *AIIIEEEE!* argue, the notion of a dual personality has effectively silenced the Chinese American writer/artist[4]: "The concept of the dual personality deprives the Chinese American and Japanese American of the means to develop their own terms" (226). Chin's play explores the space between two alien cultures, European and Chinese, to find an identity that is beholden to neither, that turns the cultural detritus and negatively charged characteristics given Chinese Americans into cause for subversion and celebration.

Dorothy MacDonald paraphrases the play as a "search for the ideal father." She sees Tam's quest for self-identity as directly linked to his ideation of fatherhood, something that can be seen in his fanatic insistence that Charlie Popcorn be Ovaltine Jack Dancer's father: "For all his self-rejection, however, Tam wishes to discover a more heroic past and identity, and believes [in] his destiny as a writer. . . . In this context, Tam's self-characterization as a linguistic orphan is made understandable" (MacDonald 111). According to the dominant image, the Chinaman in United States culture is emasculated, passive, and silent, and thus Tam admires powerful men, such as boxers, to earn respect from his own society. He comments that "Chinamen do not make good Fathers. I know, I have one" (11). When he looks to European American culture for that figure, he is verbally abused and shot in the hand by an aging and fat Lone Ranger. When he looks for a father in African American culture he finds Charlie Popcorn, who is in a sense a mirage. Ovaltine Jack Dancer had described Popcorn to Tam as a "superdad" who served as Dancer's inspiration:

> *Tam:* Ovaltine when he was a little boy in Mississippi beat up on a white boy, and you told him you all would have to leave that part of the country, and then you told him bout the welts on your back, and gettin whipped. You and the family packed up in a car. . . . You taught him "psychology" by tellin him, no matter how bad he ever got beat, or however he got beat, to always smile, stand up and say, loud, "I did enjoy the fight so very much."
>
> *Popcorn:* Where you hear all this shit, Mr Lum?
>
> *Tam:* From his book, from his mouth, from his aunt, his wife. . . .
>
> *Popcorn:* I ain't nobody's father, especially his'n. I never been no Mississippi, or done none of that. (48)

Tam discovers that Ovaltine made up Popcorn the father according to his own needs in the same way that Tam denies the existence of *his* father. The old man Tam went to fights with as a kid is never clearly defined as Tam's father. In fact, by the end of the play, Tam is alone in Kenji's kitchen invoking the power of his *grandmother's* dreams of a mythical Iron Mountain, rather than that of a paternal figure. MacDonald spells out how the mechanics of emasculation might work for Tam but misses a more radical reading of the play, a reading that, while fraught with problems, begins to articulate a possibility that escapes encapsulation within dominant culture.

Chin is merciless in analyzing Tam's inability to "find himself," to cement a stable identity within the dominant culture. He is also merciless with that culture itself. Chin assaults at least three foundations principal to the constitution of an acceptable minority position—acceptable, that is, to the dominant culture that Tam inhabits. First, Tam can never see himself reflected in the dominant media images of Chinamen that he finds in television programs such as "The Lone Ranger." The Lone Ranger, used in the play as a personification of dominant culture, occasions Tam's most powerful indoctrination into European American society by constantly degrading Chinese people and demanding that they be silent and passive in order for his drama to continue. Yet he also disrupts the apparatus by which Tam could be brought into the program's, and thus society's, imagination.

> *Lone Ranger:* Hear no evil, ya hear me? China boys, you be legendary obeyers of the law, legendary humble, legendary passive... get back to Chinatown preservin your culture. (37)

As a child, Tam tries to buy into the masked man's promise, forgetting his grandmother's recollections of the mythical Iron Horse that was to come and free the Chinese, rejecting his own cultural heritage for the mighty "Hi yo Silver, away!" As an adult, however, he finally realizes the price of that promise.

> *Tam:* He'd deafened my ear for trains all my boyhood long. (38)

While Tam sees the Lone Ranger as a senile racist who pleas with Tonto to "Kemo Sabay me" (36), to maintain his illusion of authority and dominance, Tam is still haunted by these childhood images of the legendary white man. Even when the Lone Ranger offers to make him and his childhood friend Kenji "honorary whites," an offer Tam has the presence of mind to laugh at, that image of the white man who commands respect through his aloofness still haunts Tam. Tam is able to parody the Lone Ranger ("Hi yo Silver, away!" becomes "Buck Buck Bagaw!"), to see his senility and racism for what they are, to dispense with the myth.

> *Tam:* The masked man . . . I knew him better when I never knew him at all. The Lone Ranger ain't no Chinaman, children. (38)

The second foundation, or mythology, of cultural identity that *The Chickencoop Chinaman* assaults is the notion that non-Caucasians, women, and physically disabled individuals have no one to blame but themselves for their situations and, coterminously, that any such "handicap" can be overcome by personal perseverance and "good faith." Central to the deconstruction, or, more precisely, parody, of this myth is the figure of Helen Keller. Tam and his Japanese comrade Kenji have developed a two-man tag team ritual around both Helen Keller's struggle to fit into a "normal" world and the help she received from kindly benefactors, ranging from radio ministers to the Lone Ranger. The figure of Helen Keller is important in that she represents a successful struggle against obvious birth defects—she is deaf, dumb, and blind—to become a functioning member of dominant society. She perseveres through the power of religious faith to overcome her handicaps, in the words of the radio preacher character Tam creates, "without looting . . . without violence. . . without riot" (11), without, that is, resorting to threatening or destroying white society. Instead, she becomes a mild, passive, and, most important, controllable voice for "good" causes, a supposed inspiration to minorities of all sorts. Tam and Kenji use this image to boost Tam's sagging spirits when he first arrives in Pittsburgh.

> *Tam:* If I can't talk to you, you know I . . . and I been doing a lotta talkin, Yea . . . Mumbo Jumbo. . . .
> *Kenji:* Moowahjeerfurher roar rungs!
> *Tam:* Moowahjeerfurher roar rungs?
> *Tam and Kenji:* My dear Friends! (10)

The implication in their jokes about Helen Keller is that the problems they face would actually disappear if they too would simply accept the challenge to become "white," to do the best they could, as racially handicapped individuals, to acquiesce to the established order of things. By the time they are done with their Helen Keller shtick, however, it is apparent that this choice is not a viable option.

As a result of his refusal to accept the dominant paradigms about "minority" life, Tam also has trouble assimilating into his own culture. Neither the Chinese heritage of his grandmother and her Iron Horse and mythical Iron Mountain, where the Chinese can ride the railroads, nor the heritage that posits the Chinaman as mystical and all-knowing, nor the African American culture that Tam grew up with in Oakland, California, can supply him with his missing sense of identity. He takes on some of the attributes of young black males, the handshakes and walks, while making a documentary on an African American boxer. Yet Tam rejects Popcorn's image of the "yellow Negro": and, in fact, encounters as much racial prejudice from Popcorn as he had from the Lone Ranger.

> *Popcorn:* You like music? I remember a cute little song about Chinese. American song. I still remember it: My little Hong Kong dream girl / In every dream you seem, girl . . . . You ever heard that before? (40)

While Tam does not hesitate to pass as black, while talking on the telephone, in order to manipulate Popcorn, he realizes he is not African American and merely disguises himself as such as yet another affect of one "made not born." Tam also encounters another image of assimilation in the writer Tom, who is at work on a book entitled *Soul on Rice*.

> *Tom:* I'm not prejudiced against Chinese like you. Just between you and me, brother, you have problems. (58)

Tom apparently accepts his role as a Chinese American, erasing any contradictions by claiming to "understand" his culture. Tam, however, stays angry, unwilling to accept Tom's recuperation of his Chinese heritage.

Despite the cultural traps designed to incarcerate the Chinese American in a location controllable by and subordinate to the dominant scheme, Tam manages to stay nonidentified, if identification is associated with the order and structure demanded by Western society. The final image of the play is of Tam, alone in the kitchen, affirming his Chinaman status.

> *Tam:* Now and then, I feel them old days children, the way I feel the prowl of the dogs in the night and the bugs in the leaves and the thunder in the Sierra Nevadas however far they are. The way my grandmother had an ear for trains. Listen, children, I gotta go. Ride Buck Buck Bagaw with me . . . . Listen in the kitchen for the Chickencoop Chinaman slowing on home. (66)

Tam's fascination with his nonidentity and with his lack of a birthplace, as well as his self-mocking attempts at finding a father, allows him to write his own history, to have done with the logic of origins and, instead, stick with the subversive fluidity of the word.

> *Tam:* In the beginning there was the Word! Then there was the word as if it had little lips of its own. "Chinaman" said on a little kiss. I lived the word! The word is my heritage. (6)

Tam and Kenji's wordplay forms a linguistic bond between them. Their unwillingness to take each other, or anyone else, seriously, to assimilate, or to accept mainstream culture's images of their racial heritage allows them the possibility of remaining fluid in a society that fixates on stable identities. In *The Chickencoop Chinaman*, Chin discards the icons offered to the Asian Other, disemboweling the language, and thus apparently places Tam at once both inside and outside his society. Tam pushes away from Lee's efforts to make him into a Chinese American, to typify him as the passive minority:

> *Lee:* They know all about you, mama's boys and crybabies, not a man in all your males. . . . He's talking in so many goddamn dialects and accents all mixed up at the same time. . . you might think he was a nightclub comic. What'sa wrong with your Chinatowng acka-cent, huh? (25)

Instead, severed de facto from his Chinese past, Tam takes the "master's" language and turns it on its head:

> *Tam:* And they said I had rags in my mouth, which led to ragmouth, which ended up Tampax. (25)

Rather than asserting his lost identity through a nostalgic reunification with the past, through "fighting" for something—

> *Tam:* My Country? The Alamo? And don't say my "soul" (25)

—he remains on the selvage of dominant culture, assaulting its icons, terrorizing its language:

> *Tam:* I am the result of a pile of pork chop suey thrown up into the chickencoop in the dead of night and the riot of dark birds, night cocks and insomniac nympho hens running after strange food. (8)

Tam's identity, then, comes through his ability to appropriate accents, dialects, and culture, to combine and parody forms, figures, or tropes from white culture and its Others, while also remaining distant from any one culture. In doing so, he creates a dream of moving identity. Tam's appropriation of any number of fractured identities foregrounds, at a rhetorical level, the difference between a linguistic system in which words have stable references and one in which words are involved, at their most immediate level, in a constant play that makes meaning and identity contingent upon usage and context. In this sense, Tam's inability to do anything more concrete than engage in wordplay is hardly a failure or a descent into nihilism. Rather, it is a strategy to reverse the oppression contained in Helen Keller's stuttering, the Lone Ranger's demands, and Tom's feeble appropriation of alien culture.

Tam and Kenji are always on a metasemantic as well as a semantic level. The words they speak, their Helen Keller routine, their parodic conversations with the Lone Ranger, Tam's fantasies about the Hong Kong Dream Girl, all take what have become tropes of identity and apply them within a different cultural specificity in order to pervert, perturbate, or dissolve their meaning by adding a second level of signification to their deployment. In fact, it is hard to find anything in the text that doesn't prey on a received notion or icon, a cultural understanding, or one of the characters in the play, including Tam himself.

The Chickencoop Chinaman uses textuality as a weapon against the edicts of a culture that wants to identify all Asian Americans as inheritors of a cultural tradition that, in its serenity and depth, according to Shirley Geok-lin Lim, leaves the contemporary Chinese American passive and sedate (i.e., the ideal subject for capitalist exploitation). The text dismantles the notion of the Chinaman as Western culture's mystical Other through Tam's exuberant proclivities. Tam bounces between cultural tropes, rending any affiliation with the identity European American society has disseminated. The other characters, Tom, Lee, Charlie Popcorn, and the Lone Ranger, are all representative of particular aspects of current society, tropes that present Tam with images of assimilation or acculturation. He rejects these images, or, more precisely, turns them into tropes that he can manipulate in enunciating his own sense of an indeterminate heritage.

The marginality of Tam's sense of identity can be seen in Asian American literature as something of a badge of honor, as an attempt to remain sensitive to the contradictions and difficulties encountered as an Asian American:

> Asian Americans may seem squarely placed in the so-called hegemonic stage of domination. Our literature is written primarily by American-born, American-educated Asians whose first language is English, whether we concur and collaborate or resist. The Asian American writer exists on the margins of his or her own marginal community, wedged between the hegemonic culture and the non-English-speaking communities largely unconcerned with self-definition. (Kim 1987, 88)

On the margins of society, Tam is a nomad who travels on an itinerary of his own making. He parodies both his culture and himself in order to retain his sense of being "one made, not born." The identity that emerges in the form of Tam Lum is both politically active and fractured, one that avoids essentializing "race" as a category. Tam's effort to embrace his past should not be read as an attempt to construct such a category but, rather, as an act that threatens and disables the binary cultural constructions that offer only a dissolved self or state of nonbeing as an alternative to the male European American master trope.

In certain regards Chicanos have a more clearly defined cultural presence than Chinese Americans. The term *Chicano*, according to Yolanda Broyles González, refers to people of Mexican descent living in the United States. While suggesting a Native American ancestry, it also designates a class awareness: "I deliberately avoid the use of the hegemonic term *Hispanic* because it obscures our Indian ancestry, also because it seeks to identify us with a colonial power of the sixteenth century" (González 236). The terms *Chicano* and *Chicana* are often preferred because they suggest a political identification with *la Raza* (the People): "[Chicano] is used as a mark of ethnic pride and is considered preferable by those who stress its use for reasons among which are its popular origin and the fact that it was chosen by members of the group itself" (Huerta 4).

In *Giving Up the Ghost*, there is a confrontation between the libido and the law, between two versions of desire: that which is accumulative and passive and that which is productive and active. The independently constructed desire is, in this play, the basis for a subjectivity based in part on race and in part on sexual identification. Marisa's lesbianism is deployed in the play against both European American and Chicano heterosexual norms, creating for her a positive identification, as opposed to remaining as man's objectified Other. The other character in the play, Amalia, also contorts those norms through her bisexuality. While, in terms of sexual identification, her character is more problematic than Marisa's, she resists inscription within the masculinist norms of her society. The play can be read from the perspective of a Chicana/lesbian modality, a theoretical position that remains, because of its historical condition, tentatively outside the grip of dominant culture.

Giving Up the Ghost explores both the way in which Marisa, a Chicana who "wears her toughness . . . close to the bone" (Moraga 1), understands her personal and cultural heritage and how she identifies herself sexually. The play also traces Amalia's disillusionment with and partial rejection of her heterosexual past as well as her attempts to integrate her cultural background into her current self-conception. The third person present, Corky, Marisa's girlhood self, who takes on the affectations and dress of a *cholo* ("khakis with razor-sharp creases; pressed white undershirt; hair short and slicked back" [1]), struggles with her own identification vis-à-vis white society, Protestantism, and patriarchy. The first act takes place in 1980 for Amalia and Marisa and 1963 for Corky, the second still in 1980 for the two older women but in 1969 for Corky. The play is constructed around these three seemingly separate narratives, or monologues, which only seldom intersect.

> The lighting should give the impression that the actors are within hearing range of one another; that they in fact *know* what the other is saying (thinking), even when there is no obvious response from the "listener." (1)

In the second act, Marisa and Amalia do interact—apparently as lovers—but they never engage in traditional dialogue, never create a "fourth wall" between themselves and the viewing audience. Moraga designates "the People, those viewing the performance," as the fourth character in her list of characters. Given, however, that the audience exists in real time, the mechanisms that would create illusionism, or a fourth wall, are incapacitated. The play makes no distinction between real time and diegetic time.

The three onstage characters thus have dual roles: one with the audience and the other with one another. Through these roles, the play critiques the cultural oppression of Chicanas and analyzes individual and cultural problems of lesbian identification. Corky, at ages eleven and seventeen, struggles to find a position within her society. An outsider in terms of both race and sex, she constantly struggles against a society that finds sufficient cause to condemn her on either ground. As a Chicana, she is marginalized by the "paddys," the neighborhood Protestants, and their strange religious practices.

> *Corky:* Lisa [the girl down the street] be hassling me and my sister
>   Patsy all the time
>   tell us how we wernt really Christians cuz cath-lics
>   worshipped the virgin mary or somet'ing. (9)

While she finds warmth, reassurance, and love from her own mother—

> *Corky:* it was so nice to hear her voice
>   so warm like she loved us a lot
>   'n' that night
>   being cath-lic felt like my mom
>   real warm 'n' dark 'n' kind (13)

—the cold austerity of Lisa's religion, its imperious sense of privilege, drives Corky away, marginalizing her even as she tries to assert the strength she receives from her mother. After losing an argument with Lisa about the relative merits of Catholicism versus Protestantism and flying into a blind rage that leads to her censorship by Lisa's mother, she learns to hide her feelings when in mainstream culture. Her experience with the paddys drives her inward, forcing her to internalize her rage, repressing her own sense of culture:

> *Corky:* As the door shuts in front of my face
>   I vow I'll never make a mistake like that again . . .
>   I'll never show anybody how mad I can get. (19)

Thus, early in life, she finds out how little Anglo European society wants her around, unless she is willing to reject her Chicano background.

Corky also discovers her sexual difference as well as her racial difference at an early age:

Corky: The smarter I get the older I get the meaner I get
tough a tough cookie My mom calls me. (4)

Yvonne Yarbro-Bejarano identifies two primary subject positions open to women in Chicano theater, positions that, unfortunately, seem to be prevalent in any patriarchal order.[5] *La Malinche* and her counterpart, *La Virgen,* represent women as either, like Eve, responsible for the postlapsarian world or, like the Virgin Mary, as immaculate, unfathomable, forever idolized as otherworldly. According to legend, *La Malinche* was sold by her mother into slavery to Tenepal and then again to Cortez. She also sold out her people in return for sexual favors and, as a result, produced the mestizo, or half-breed race. She also represents, in contemporary mythology, the whore or desire out of control. Conversely, *La Virgen* is passivity exemplified. Resigned and self-effacing, she is defenseless against *El Chingón,* the macho male.[6] In between reverence and disgust, Yarbro-Bejarano suggests, the Chicana who questions her role runs the risk of being rejected by the Chicano community, and she must prove her commitment to *La Raza* by maintaining her sexual and social subordination to her culture's heterosexual norms.[7] According to Nancy Saporta Sternbach, however, Moraga uses the image of *Malinche*[8] to rewrite the myth, to move from a historically powerless position to the articulation of an identity that frees her from the inherent contradiction in the dilemma of *Malinche* (of being the "great Mother" and the traitor, or whore):

What makes Moraga's assessment different is that in this case the daughter, in turn, is accused of betraying her race by choosing the sex of her mother as the object of her love. . . . While other writers focus on Malinche herself as if they were her actual daughters, Moraga prefers to direct her analysis toward Malinche's mother, likening her to her own. (54)

Malinche becomes a symbol of Moraga's attempts to rewrite her own history outside both dominant culture and her own culture's inscription of woman as mother, whore, traitor, or angel.

Moraga's fears of inscription are well founded. The Chicano Cultural Nationalists of the 1960s and 1970s felt that Chicanas who agitated for equal sex/gender roles were in fact selling out the movement by creating a division within it. Chicanas were expected to be subservient to and supportive of their male counterparts; that is, they were expected to remain in their traditional roles and question neither the family structure nor their function in it.

> Chicanas who question traditional gender roles and attempt to organize their desire independently run the risk of being labeled *malinchistas* (traitors). They are perceived as corrupted by "foreign" or "bourgeois" influences that threaten to destroy their people. Under the pressure of this conflation of class, racial, and sexual betrayal, the Chicana proves her fidelity to her people by means of a sexual commitment to the Chicano male, "putting the male first" within the heterosexual structures of the family and the culture. (Yarbro-Bejarano 1986a, 393)

The Chicana was thus caught in her traditional sociosexual position by the heterosexual family structure.

Corky, it seems, is in trouble with her role in both Chicano and dominant culture at a very early age:

> *Corky:* Funny now when I think about how little I was
>   at the time and a girl
>   but in my mind I was big 'n' tough 'n' a dude
>   in my mind. (5)

Her dream is to be a man. She carries a blade, runs with a Chicano, pretending to "capture chicks 'n' hold 'em up . . . make 'em take their clothes off" (5), and idolizes the *batos*, who "get all cut up at the weddings / getting their rented tuxes all bloody" (4). The *batos* have agency, have a certain social legitimacy, at least within Chicano culture (that they are erased in dominant culture is, of course, an issue as well), something she is denied as a Chicana. Her identification with the *batos* alienates her from the world around her, a paradoxical effect, since it is that identification that gives her a sense of self. With no positive model to select, she resists the Chicana role. To identify herself as a *bato* is to refuse to comply with either her role as Chicana within that culture or the role of passive, silent outsider in dominant culture.[9]

She never escapes, however, never becomes a man:

> *Corky:* I never could
>   quite
>   pull it off
>   always knew I was a girl. (6)

The ideal of having and holding an individual subject position within society eludes Corky; she is condemned to inscription as an object. As much as she fights her role, she is brought back, always reinscribed as woman, man's Other. The male dominance of her world comes clear to her one day when her father makes sexual advances to her mother in the kitchen:

> *Corky:* Cheeezus! I coulda died!
>   I musta been only 'bout nine or so but I got that tingling
>   tú sabes that now I know what it means. (29)

Finally, as if her inculcation into patriarchy was not always already complete, Corky is raped by a worker at school. Her rape answers any questions she had about her expected role in society.

> *Corky:* I never cried as he shoved the thing
>   into what was supposed to be a mouth
>   with no teeth
>   with no hate
>   with no voice
>   only a hole. A Hole
>   . . . HE MADE ME A HOLE! (43)

Maria Herrera-Sobek sees Corky's rape as the

> consequence and process of making, engendering, a group of hu-
> mans—women. In this process of en-gendering, fabricating, that
> is, making a gender, the end result is a hole and absence. . . domi-
> nated by ingrained patriarchal vectors where the Name of the
> Father is Law, and years of socialization to obey the Father's Law
> transforms the female subject into a quavering accomplice in her
> own rape. (172–73)

Her dreams of subjectivity, encoded as they are in the framework of
gender, of being a *bato* and having the corresponding social and societal privileges, are shattered by the rape, for it forces her to account
for the fact that, in the symbolic register of the Father, she is absent.
Not coincidentally, Corky disappears from the stage after this realization, but the consequences of her experiences continue in Marisa.

In terms of ego psychology, Marisa must bear the burden of her
childhood in her current life. The anguish and pain Corky felt after
being raped manifests in Marisa as a sense of betrayal. The fights
Corky started because she could not accept her passive role still play
out their drama in her adult life:

> What is betrayal?. . . It's about a battle I will never win and never
> stop fighting. The dick beats me every time. (8)

If Marisa's ironic comment about her relationship with patriarchal
culture is read alongside the dedication to the first act—

> I am, in fact,
> *not* trapped
> which brings me to the question of prisons
> politics
> sex
>
> (2)

—Marisa's character can be read as existing simultaneously inside
and outside dominant culture. Her lesbian identification partially

compensates for her rejection of the traditional position of Chicana, by offering an agency that might not otherwise be available:

> I never wanted to be a man
> I only wanted a woman to want me that bad.
>
> (14)

As a lesbian, she can fashion a sense of subjectivity; even so, the scars from her encounters with the patriarchy when she was Corky do not disappear so easily. As a Chicana, she is still constructed as an object by dominant culture, still expected or required to be *La Malinche* or *La Virgen*, and, while she has identified herself outside the heterosexual economy, she is still marked by her understanding of what society expects of her:

> I don't regret it
> I don't regret nuthin.
> He only convinced me of my own name.
> From an early age you learn to live with it,
> being a woman.
>
> (43)

The question of "prisons, politics, sex" could be read, in this context, in two different ways. The triad could be seen as either mutual accomplices in the incarceration of Marisa into the object position in a heterosexual discourse or as two lines of flight from prison: one through the active assertion of her Chicana subjectivity in a world that designates women as objects, the other through her sexuality. Patriarchal culture does not posit a position for the lesbian, since women are seen as objects of exchange, not as agents. Marisa then exists in the "dark area" excluded from the male economy, an area that, once inhabited, can of course no longer be "dark" but, rather, outside and therefore a constant threat to her society's definition of female as *La Chingada* (the fucked one). Yet Moraga's play does not simply leave Marisa and Amalia isolated in an exclusionary world. Norma Alarcón suggests that *Giving Up the Ghost* "puts into play the concepts 'man' and 'woman' (and the parodic 'butch/femme'), with the intuitive knowledge that they operate in our subjectivities, so that it is difficult to analyze them" (156). By doing so, Moraga confuses the rigidity of the Law that demands a normative man-woman dyad and complicates simple identifications.

For Teresa de Lauretis, the change that occurs in Amalia and Marisa is not from female object to female subject but, rather, at a more abstract level, from female to feminist. The female, identified by biological and sexual differences and constituted through dominant cultural apparatus, is stuck within the ideology of her society and thus constituted as object by the same processes that males are constituted as subject. Hailed by ideology and written into the cultural imaginary, the female, while able to assert her Otherness, is nonetheless trapped as she is interpellated into the dominant order. The feminist subject, however, is not identified solely as man's Other but, according to de Lauretis, as "at the same time inside and outside the ideology of gender, and conscious of being so, conscious of that pull, that division, that doubled vision" (1987, 10). Thus, the feminist subject can assert her own desire without first putting it in the context of Oedipus.

Crucial to the inhabitability of this subject position is de Lauretis's distinction between hom(m)osexuality and homosexuality. In this visual pun, de Lauretis conflates the Greek and Latin *homo* ("Man" in one and "Same" in the other) with the French *Homme* ("Man"), a pun that Luce Irigaray also makes. She thus distinguishes between hom(m)sexuality that is the same as man, or sexual indifference, and homosexuality, or lesbian and/or gay sexuality (de Lauretis 1988, 156). Lesbian identification can be separated from male/female subject/object relationships and ideology, creating a transposition of desire that both avoids and subverts the dominant, ghosted desire:

> The struggle with language . . . is a struggle to transcend both gender and "sex" and recreate the body other-wise: to see it perhaps as monstrous, or grotesque, or mortal, or violent, and certainly also sexual, but with a material and sensual specificity that will resist phallic idealization and render it accessible to women in another sociosexual economy. (167)

de Lauretis re-visions the continuum of desire that appears in *Giving Up the Ghost* as a flow that bypasses the oedipal narrative, and, instead, establishes a network of objects that are free to desire without first constituting a subjectivity in terms of the law of fathers: "The play itself has moved away from any simple opposition of 'lesbian' to 'heterosexual' and into the conceptual and experiential continuum of a female, Chicana subjectivity from where the question of lesbian desire must finally be posed" (175). The residual of these flows is a lesbian subjectivity that, rather than remaining fixed in an economy of domination and Otherness, maintains its fluidity, forms a nomadic existence that can wander along lines of escape, or flows of desire, without regard for a heterosexual affiliation. According to de Lauretis, both Marisa and Amalia represent different stages of the motile subject; both make an initial escape from dominant society.

Marisa and Amalia can thus escape through each other's seduction through creating dual subject positions rather than a subject/object field of domination.[10] In doing so, they formulate a lesbian subjectivity outside oedipal narratives, a tactic that, for Marisa at least, gains her a space that can disavow the self-hatred that plagued Corky and that potentially avoids the (holy) triadic economy of the Ghost. The element of confusion that enters into the play through this relationship is due to the fact that identification as lesbian or heterosexual is difficult at best: "It is as if Moraga knows that in 'real' life these two women may not be able to speak to each other directly in any effective way, thus we must enter their sociosymbolic lives, in a dialogue that is always a near miss" (Alarcón 155). While "feminist" desire (desire outside the Law of the Father—de Lauretis) appears in *Giving Up the Ghost*, it is not in and of itself an answer to the question of ethnic identity that also runs through the play. Marisa and Amalia cannot simply be identified as feminists, nor do they easily fit into the Chicano culture as a whole. Between the two poles, then, there is a double identification, a constant pull that seems to threaten the stability of any one('s) position.

Giving Up the Ghost does not posit a simple lesbian/heterosexual polarity. The play further complicates sexual identification through the character of Amalia. On the one hand, Amalia corresponds to *La Chingada*; she is involved with a man who, after he dies, leaves her alone and forlorn:

> When I learned of Alejandro's death,
> I died too, weeks later.
> I just started bleeding and the blood wouldn't stop,
> not until his ghost had passed through me.
>
> (27)

But, on the other, she is Marisa's current lover, and, as her feelings for Marisa trigger memories of the dead Alejandro, she actively constructs her new role. Again, the question must be asked: If dominant discourse constructs only two possibilities, subject or object, where does Amalia fit? With *La Chingada*? If so, how can she be involved with Marisa? As a lesbian? But she defines her relationship with men completely different from how Marisa does, for example. She feels that Alejandro was reborn inside of her and that it is he who makes love to Marisa:

> I can' say exactly why or how I knew this, except again for the smell, the unmistakable
> Smell of the sex of the man
> as if we had just made love
> el olor estaba en el aire
> alrededor de la cama
> and coming from my lips was *his* voice
> "Ay mi Marisa! ¡Te deseo! ¡Te deseo!"
>
> (28)

Her inordinate position, like Marisa's lesbianism, escapes the heterosexual norm, not by asserting an elided position but, rather, by sliding between discourses, between sexual economies, equivocating with her sexual identification, providing another line of escape from the dominant order. Amalia's relationship to her own sexuality somewhat problematizes this escape, however, for it is unclear whether she sees Marisa as a woman or as a male substitute. The former condition would confirm a lesbian/bisexual duality, one that problematizes its own binary dynamic because of the slippage in both terms. The latter condition, however, problematizes their flight, for it seems that Amalia is always hoping for something else from Marisa, something she is not. Marisa muses, alone at the end of the play:

> If only sex coulda saved us. . . .
> I am preparing myself for the worst,
> so I cling to her in my heart,
> my daydream with pencil in my mouth,
> when I put my fingers
> to my own
> forgotten places.
>
> (56–58)

Indeed, Amalia's heterosexuality ultimately causes her to leave. Situated between lesbian and heterosexual identification, she remains in neither position. Amalia's departure creates for Marisa another barrier that prevents her from taking a place in society.

> *Marisa:* It's like making familia from scratch
> each time all over again. . . with strangers
> if I must.
> If I must, I will. (58)

Yet, it is her ability to "make familia from scratch," to create a family according to her wishes rather than the dictates of a society, that allows her to survive and to create a place for herself.

Beyond this account of character and narrative, there is another level on which *Giving Up the Ghost* plays out its drama(s), another level at which Marisa's status can be reconfigured as something other than victim. If the title can be taken as that which names or designates the principles of organization within the text, if reading the title can be akin to reading the foundational structure of a text, then the ghost that is given up is particularly indicative of the text's desiring economies. The ghost could, of course, be Marisa's past life as Corky and her past associations with violence, race hatred, and misogyny.

Read another way, the ghost could be that of the Christian Trinity, the missing link between the Father and the Son. The Holy Ghost, the spirit that links fathers and sons, could be read as an image of the prescriptive form of desire, the desire that signifies a lack, that is tied to the order of fathers. In *Giving Up the Ghost*, this order is represented in terms of both European American and Chicano social structures. In this order, the man controls or at least designates the flow of desire, one that characteristically constitutes the male as subject and the female as object, both of desire and of possession. The *batos* and their knives and bloody tuxedos, the paddys and their austere churches and spoiled children, the worker who rapes Corky, and, finally, the father who fucks Corky's mother at the breakfast table are all subjects, all given fixed and secure positions within discourse from which to possess or desire women. They represent a grid of control wherein desire can flow only according to the needs of the dominant order, an order of fathers and sons that can imagine woman only as exchange object, never as desiring subject, for a desiring woman threatens to disrupt the patriarchal order.[11] In its compulsory heterosexual state, tied to the Father, the Son, and the Holy Ghost, desire is a frozen stream, rigid and unobtainable from outside its order. Indeed, it can only be its own ghost, prescribed by and beholden to the law of the father, to the machinations of an oedipal complex. The ghost that inscribes this kind of desire, that passes between the two alternatives, father or son, defining the world as it shifts from side to side, is finally given up. Along with it, however, the certainty of life under its sign is given up. Yet in its place is, for Marisa and Tam Lum, a "fractured" self, one that can be in more than one place at a time, that can recognize the impossibility of a single identity as well as the consequences of living outside the dominant cultural paradigm.

Within these texts, a politics based on the plurivalence of identity within the rubric "ethnic" emerges. The radical ethnic subject posited by *The Chickencoop Chinaman* in the form of Tam Lum, for example, problematizes the notion of that subject for, quite simply, Tam never actually assumes any sort of identity for any length of time. He does not deny the various influences from which he was formed, both in terms of his own culture and in terms of the ethnicity that dominant society imposed on him as a further mechanism of psychic slavery. In another context, the same argument could be made for Marisa in *Giving Up the Ghost*. Should she be defined as Chicana, as woman, as lesbian? Each characterization limits her in a different way, prevents her from establishing herself because of the restrictions each category demands. Consequently, what becomes apparent is that there are a number of positions already within "ethnicity," that the monolithic use of the term may in fact satisfy the humanist need to delineate an other-than-dominant category through which to silence minority discourse.

These two texts move toward a land of created histories and identities wherein "History" as a master-narrative appears as a suspect category. Implicit in this move is the end of master-tropes and categories such as Identity, Ethnicity, and History, categories previously legitimated as hegemonic structures based on these tropes' and categories' true and correct relation to a Real, or dominant, status. The humanist agenda entails a claim for universality, a process that subsequently defines its Others in terms of a particular master-narrative, a correct interpretation, or a canonical standard—all variations on the Platonic structure of a "one and a many." This structure engenders a notion of ethnic identity as it corresponds to or differs from the hegemonic perspective, a structure that emphasizes the "majority" position as the correct one and the "minority" as but a pale shadow of its better. Difference, in terms of both race and gender, is similarly measured in terms of distance from an essentialized norm.

Another history of ethnicity can be constructed, however, one that not only differs from its dominant corollary, but "defers," puts aside, deflects, the postulates of the dominant order and plays on its meanings, its structures, and its hegemony.[12] The "différance" built into this notion of the play of meanings with ethnic positions radically upsets the state of balance central to the humanist universe. This second history also calls into question the notion of a unified, self-willing subject predicated on universal notions. The "Man" can only speak for the human condition as a whole when the differences—material, racial, gendered—within that condition are collapsed into a one-dimensional perspective. When the voice of the Other begins to speak, however, the contradictions, elisions, and inconsistencies within the ideology of "Man" become apparent, if "only" because these voices speak of, among other things, class structure, sexual difference, and racial inequality.

What appears is a doubled movement within each articulation of the sign of difference, for within each is both the containment and the disruption of that sign: "Current language use signifies the difference between cultures and their possession of power, spelling out the distance between subordinate and superordinate, between bondsman and lord in terms of their 'race'" (Gates 1985, 6). Perturbing the sign at every turn is the consequential and worldly mode that signs perforce effect: "To use contemporary theories of criticism to explicate these modes of inscription is to demystify large and obscure ideological relations and, indeed, theory itself" (6). Articulating ethnicity produces a series of questions that can be addressed by constant referral to the historical and worldly condition of ethnicity. In this sense, ethnicity does not signify a disappearance into a world of humanist plurality or indifference but, rather, reasserts a historically grounded notion of theory—theory tied directly to, and contingent on, political interests and investments. In the words of Barbara Christian: "My 'method' . . . is not fixed but relates to what I read and to the historical context of the writers I read *and* to the many critical activities in which I am engaged" (62). Christian's assessment of the necessity to contextualize any question of identity within history and within politics is a valuable response to the ennui and defeatism that often accompanies theories of the "end" of the Eurocentric, humanist universe, in that it suggests that the "struggle" with "ideology" takes place both in theory and in daily relationships.

One question which must be addressed is the presence of a dominant power structure, and the presumptions of that power structure. In the context of the United States, the cultural power structure is one which is dominated by the ideology of a specifically white, Eurocentric, specifically capitalist establishment. (Daryl Chin, 167)

Daryl Chin places the question of ethnic identity directly in line with questions of power, of economics, and of capitalism in such a way that identity cannot be separated from political status. Politics, in this configuration, implies to some degree a shift from attempting to define power within an ontological scheme to accessing power as a deliberate strategy without necessarily needing to first "survey all the threads" of that particular instance of power, without having to construct power as something to be seized from particular sites or apparatus, or without having to rely on a "party politics" mentality to liberate or enslave.

Yet the transfer of theoretical notions developed in the context of European American discourse to ethnic theater can be readily rejected as an example of a European American critic "picking up the white man's burden." In "Can the Subaltern Speak?" Gayatri Spivak argues that to invoke the ethnic Other as a genuflection ignores the sociopolitical realities of global capitalism and its compliance with nation-state ideology. Furthermore, to ignore the effects of those realities on traditionally underrepresented groups (or subalterns) is a way consequently to cause their continued disappearance. In constructing "the Other" as a convenient alibi onto which can be transferred the inadequacies and anxieties of a particular cultural perspective, the problem of representation and identity is not solved: "The subaltern cannot speak. There is no virtue in global laundry lists with 'woman' as a pious item" (Spivak 308). It is not enough simply to invoke, or "quote," subaltern performance practices so as to "become global," as certain contemporary Western practitioners would imagine.[13] Indeed, can a notion of theater that does not give equal space for ethnic voices to speak on their own terms actually be considered heterogeneous?

Historically, Western intellectuals, writers, and politicians have often spoken for and in the place of the subaltern—however that person is identified. Under the ruse of explaining their deficiencies and shortcomings, the subaltern is effectively silenced. For example, in his famous study *Orientalism*, Edward Said demonstrates how Western attitudes toward the Middle East consistently construct that region as a mysterious Other to a "normal," normative Europe, a relationship dependent on the notion of "Europe" as a standard by which the rest of the world is measured: "Here, of course, is the most familiar of Orientalism's themes—since the Orientals cannot represent themselves, they must therefore be represented by others who know more about Islam than Islam knows about itself" (97). The effects of such "Orientalism," Said argues, are that the "East" is "taken care of" in a paternalistic manner, is the source of unknown terror and threat to the stable West, or is a land of mystery and intrigue. When combined, these attitudes prevent any effective understanding of the situation and problems of countries outside Europe; that is, "the Orient" appears geographically, economically, religiously, and sociopolitically only in relation to the "Occident." For Said, prime examples of Orientalism are found in the treatment of the Palestinian people as well as in the latent racism of the recent Persian Gulf war. The tendency in the West to look at other cultures, societies, and peoples as fundamentally different is predicated upon an imperative that demands that difference be explained in terms of the Same. Indeed, people should view with suspicion any "European American" theorist who considers the writings of other ethnic groups in the context of a potentially hegemonic umbrella such as "post-structuralist theater," particularly since such a project can too easily become yet another instance of the universalizing theorist who addresses his or her audience as "we," designates him- or herself as "I," and forgets to problematize his or her own imperialist heritage.

Yet, throughout this project, "I" hope to "forget my umbrella"[14] by rejecting the "Man" who structures too much theater history, criticism, and theory. "A critical difference from myself means that I am not i, am within and without i. I/i can be I or i, you and me both involved. . . . The differences made *between* entities comprehended as absolute presences . . . are an outgrowth of a dualistic system of thought peculiar to the Occident" (Trinh 90). To take seriously the significance and potential of the "end of Man" and, furthermore, to attempt to build a coalition politics as a part of a post-structured theater that is not simply suggestive of the world of the margin but also incorporates it as an operational matrix may be a first step in this direction. In a sense, "my" discourse, the discourse of the European

American academic, is already over at the moment it approaches ethnicity, already has nothing more to say, if to speak is to attempt to tell the truth about the object of analysis. Yet this admission too might be a ruse to avoid confronting the limits, or margins, of the post-structured stage (which is, by definition, "at the margins"). Avoiding the question of ethnicity, coloniality, or imperialism when suggesting that the "so-called humanist" stage is not all that it is meant to be only perpetuates its universalizing mystique, albeit on another level.[15] My intention in this chapter is not to describe a history of ethnic theaters or to provide lists of dramatic texts that are certifiably "correct" for the purposes of this study or even to apologize for their inclusion, or my presence, although certainly I try to be aware of the various difficulties that arise.

In initiating a discussion of ethnic theater, I am attempting to situate my own theoretical heritage in its historical moment, a heritage that signals a complex intersection of imperialist and anti-imperialist tendencies, one that is marked by a certain institutional privilege, certainly, but one that also attempts to understand that privilege in its fullest possible significance. In this sense, the work of the anthropologist Clifford Geertz, and in particular his book *Works and Lives: The Anthropologist as Author*, is particularly useful in providing a metastructure to this chapter:

> "Being there" authorially, palpably on the page, is in any case as difficult a trick to bring off as "being there" personally, which after all demands at the minimum hardly more than a travel booking and permission to land; a willingness to endure a certain amount of loneliness, invasion of privacy, and physical discomfort; a relaxed way with odd growths and unexplained fevers; a capacity to stand still for artistic insults, and the sort of patience that can support an endless search for invisible needles in infinite haystacks. And the authorial sort of being there is getting more difficult all the time. (24)

To raise the voice of the Other is to bring to full accounting the theoretical perspective generated in the previous three chapters. This critique must also come out of and speak to and with the position(s) and address(es) that I adopt so far in this project. Geertz's discomfort with the "authorial" means inherited from Western intellectual history of engaging a text is a point well taken when thought of in terms of what it means to let a text speak in the context of another text.

As a starting point for a "post-imperialist" perspective, then, the phrases "to speak for" and "to speak with" need to be differentiated. "To speak for," in this case, would be to imagine that my voice as critic enables me to take some sort of position as mediator between the text and an audience, a relationship that not only replicates the manner in which "we in the West" have always talked about other cultures and peoples but that also defines those peoples and cultures in terms of the West: "A conversation of 'us' with 'us' about 'them' is a conversation in which 'them' is silenced. 'Them' always stands on the other side of the hill, naked and speechless, barely present in its absence" (Trinh 67). Slipping into the type of theater anthropology that has become popular in recent years is, in this arrangement, simply a more seductive and subtle colonization process: "The anthropologist-nativist who speaks 'about them' and 'for them' is like the man who 'strikes a mouse with a stick he doesn't want to soil!' " (67).

"To speak with," on the other hand, would be to actually listen and respond within the context of the particular text, keeping in mind that any context that the theorist enters is, of course, irreparably reconfigured in and by the theorist's presence. I have not intended these readings to replace or explain any text but, rather, to map certain connections between the critiques developed in the three preceding chapters and the ethnic-identified discourse currently generated by a variety of theoretical and theatrical voices. Indeed, Audre Lorde has said as much in the context of the white feminist movement's ignorance of women of color in the 1960s and 1970s (and 1980s). In "An Open Letter to Mary Daly," Lorde both specifically responds to Daly's book *Gyn/Ecology* and, more generally, emphasizes the difference between speaking for and speaking with another person: "Do you ever really read the work of black women? Did you ever read my words, or did you merely finger through them for quotations which you thought might valuably support an already-conceived idea?" (95). Rather, a different sort of relationship to the text needs to be found in order to avoid similar mistakes.

The politics that arises from the recognition of a difference within ethnicity itself also entails a rejection of the humanist standard. "In my own tradition, theorists have turned to the black vernacular tradition . . . to isolate the signifying black difference through which to theorize about the so-called discourse of the Other" (Gates 1985, 16). The movement in the theater of color is from an aesthetic based on one major structure or discourse from which all Others are disseminated to one based on heterogeneity, not a multiplicity within the one but, rather, separate specific politics predicated on the historical experience and worldly needs of its participants.

> Categorizations of cultural enterprise which have dominated discourse over the past century have been usurped, without having been replaced; . . . information retention systems have made available more information than can be understood by any individual; . . . socio-economic dependencies are now inextricably bound while geopolitical structures remain demarcated, maintaining a rigid definition of boundary and border. (Daryl Chin 175)

The ensuing strategic identity becomes a political choice, rather than a biological or essentialist necessity, to be deployed in the context of external relations rather than in the fabrication of an ideological, psychic nomenclature. "Race has become a trope of ultimate, irreducible difference between cultures, linguistic groups, or adherents of specific belief systems which . . . also have fundamentally opposed economic interests. Race is the ultimate trope of difference because it is so very arbitrary in its application" (Gates 1985, 5). Within the contexts in which these two plays exist, there is a textuality of ethnicity; between each context, there is a textuality of identity that countermands dominant textuality practice by perturbating the sensibility required to maintain an Otherness.

Unless one understands the necessity of a practice of language which remains, through its signifying operations, a process constantly unsettling the identity of meaning and speaking/writing subject, a process never allowing I to fare without non-I. Trying to find the other by defining otherness or by explaining the other through laws and generalities is, as Zen says, like beating the moon with a pole or scratching an itching foot from the outside of a shoe. . . . In writing close to the other of the other, I can only choose to maintain a self-reflexively critical relationship toward the material, a relationship that defines both the subject written and the writing subject, undoing the I while asking "what do I want wanting to *know* you or me?" (Trinh 76)

CHAPTER 5

Writing beyond the Vanishing Point: Theorizing Theater

I've never been sure about the need for literary criticism. If a work is immediate enough, alive enough, the proper response isn't to be academic, to write about it, but to use it, to go on. By using each other, each other's texts, we keep on living, imagining, making, fucking, and we fight this society of death.

—Kathy Acker

The future of theatre is in philosophy.

—Bertolt Brecht

Somebody once asked me, not in a very congenial way, why I picked a collection of texts that range from the obscure to the unknown. Why not contend with theater's established stars? Furthermore, I was asked, why use theories, developed for the most part in narrative and literary contexts, to approach the theater, to approach performance and theatricality, which are, after all, at least in this country, perhaps the least theorized aesthetic modes imaginable? Without a doubt, this entire line of questioning strikes me as silly. The study of marginality in literary discourse is well established in English and comparative literature departments; a glance through any of the numerous academic journals in the field suggests that the theater remains impervious to questions of authority and marginality (in Derrida's sense) and maintains, for the most part, the same rigorously exclusionary precepts that contemporary theory threw out twenty years ago. Fortunately, this condition seems to be changing, notably through the work of Elin Diamond, Herbert Blau, Timothy Murray, and others. Yet the question remains, especially in the context of textuality: Why these texts? Why this theory?

The nine texts I include in the preceding chapters have, perhaps, two central influences, or antecedents. Certainly, they represent a theater connected to the political and social struggles of the 1960s, 1970s, and 1980s in the United States and Europe. Rather than reflecting this influence solely on a diegetic level, however—although *Giving Up the Ghost* and *The Chickencoop Chinaman* do portray actual struggles—these plays' basic distrust of institutional or traditional theatrical apparatus appears in their structures. For the most part, the theater that emerges from the general sensibility of these texts, a theater that, for lack of a better name, I am calling "post-structured," problematizes its ties to the principles and aesthetics that have defined the major dramatic canon since the advent of realism. The ingrained suspicion and rejection of traditional social structures, inherited in part from modernism, is accompanied by an increased awareness of the philosophical implications of recent discourses on the construction and usage of texts and of the difficulties inherent in the assemblage of textuality. Furthermore, the post-structured stage can be differentiated from the historical avant-garde in that there is in post-structuralism a strong awareness of the failure of modernity's universalizing perspective (as characterized by both "Enlightenment" and "anti-Enlightenment" thinking) to provide a basis for either critique or positive social action. The post-structured stage elevates "play" and "theatricality" as viable philosophical and theatrical modes and inculcates the stage with a heterogeneity that is recklessly calculated to disrupt the authoritarian vestiges within theory itself. As such, the post-structured stage remains on the selvage of continual disappearance, for, in resisting its own institutionality, it pulls the rug out from under the foundations, as it were, of aesthetic, or canon-forming, processes.

In the past thirty years a number of artists have raised the stakes on representation by rejecting its traditional components, foundations, institutions, and apparatus and have vigorously explored alternative venues, modes, and processes (e.g., body art, dance, happenings, action paintings, installations, etc.). Performance art's willingness to jettison categorical notions of what constitutes art, to explode the boundaries of performance and everyday life, and to pillage other art forms to find useful techniques and "objects" challenges theater to do the same. As such, performance art (a category that is necessarily vague) facilitates an entirely new set of possibilities for theater, if only by way of example for those practitioners who notice. Within the representational networks in which the institution of theater is immured, performance art has opened hitherto unnoticed spaces. Through questioning the notion of character as a unified self, disrupting the foundations of a humanist universe by not basing narrative on Man, and dissolving the difference between illusion and everyday life, these plays problematize the naturalist/realist theater.

The authors I discuss herein are first and foremost intent on creating their own textualities, contexts, and mechanisms. Cherríe Moraga, for example, situates her play within the context of Chicana theater and lesbian desire, not as oddities within the mainstream but, rather, as foundations upon which the text proceeds. Yet these "foundations" themselves are, on one level, perturbations of foundation qua foundation, a reversal that in a sense makes the whole discussion of "origin" or "foundation" nonsensical. Rainer Werner Fassbinder's texts, while written from a different cultural location and with accordingly different investments from Moraga's, are concerned with similar perturbations and, indeed, go so far as to suggest the processes by which nonsense converts to fascism. Furthermore, the differences between Moraga, a Chicana lesbian living in the United States under a late-capitalist regime, and Fassbinder, a gay male who lived on the sexual fringes of the German Federal Republic, do not necessarily collapse their projects into one unified margin simply because, at one level, their textual projects are related. In fact, the notion of a "margin" and "center" is itself problematic in a world of disappearing origins. What does it mean to have a center, especially if the illusion of origins has always been to conceal its own politics? In this sense, the diversity and apparent incongruity of the authors I include in this project are imperative to avoiding the sort of reading that simply reestablishes its center on grounds either deemed more politically fashionable or that simply ignore the question completely.

As a result, the notion of theater I have tried to develop herein problematizes its own categorization—which makes the need for theory, or at least the suitability for what these days is considered "theory," and in particular "post-structuralist theory," increasingly important to the theater, if only to keep up with the proliferation of new theatrical modes and textualities. For example, what determines cate-gorization, how is a director/reader/actor/audience to understand or "interpret" a text, or, for that matter, what categorizes theater, what makes it appear as a "genre" in the first place? Is theater definable by its institutional apparatus, does it "take (a) place," as Julia Kristeva would say, by subscribing to certain normative ideological perspec-tives? Wallace Shawn's and Caryl Churchill's plays suggest this sort of affiliation with the State apparatus. Or is it defined by its theatricality, which would positively open up "the field of drama" (to use Martin Esslin's phrase) to all sorts of unheard-of perspectives and excesses, both good and bad, as seen in both performance art and, more important (for theatricality), post-structuralist thought? "To hide, to show, that is the heart of theatricality. The modernity of our fin-de-siècle is due to this: there is nothing to be replaced, no lieuten-ancy is legitimate, or else all are; the replacing—therefore the mean-ing—is itself only a substitute for displacement" (Lyotard 1976, 105). As I mentioned in the first chapter, theatricality has, in post-structur-alist thought, become perhaps the central operative, a metalepsis that allows the theorist to be in two places at once, as it were—to be, with Frank Chin's Tam Lum, both inside and outside culture at any given moment; to be, with Kathy Acker, "in the realm of the senseless."

The best argument for theory in the context of theater studies comes in this very idea: the dual movement on the stage, of not taking (a) place in the sense of disrupting or problematizing the se-mantic register of dominant discourse by being in (more than) two places at once, as it were, almost necessitates a theoretical question-ing at every point that the theatrical appears. This constant need for interrogation is what Blau is on to when he states: "Theater is theory, or a shadow of it. . . . In the act of seeing, there is already theory" (1982, 1). Theater, or theatricality, is not, then, something that should really be taken for granted; the conditions that impel it are them-selves always suspect, or should be so, if theater is to escape its own institutionality. The equivocation of the theatrical is always opposed to the institutionality of theater, to the sense-making apparatus that would confine every meaning to some sort of signifier-signified equivalence. Because of this opposition, theater exists already in theory, in the realm of what was once considered philosophy, until the duplicitousness of the theater made such categorical distinctions impossible.

Yet, for all this, theory has been accepted (marginally) into the world of theater studies only after facing the greatest resistances, ones that are still present. Despite the almost universal acceptance of theory, whether it be post-structuralist or other, in comparative literature, French, and English departments, theater studies has resisted, as if to express some anxiety about the consequences for theory onstage, the notion that any theatrical moment is also theoretical, if only because present in the act of seeing, as Blau has argued, there is an infinite regression of appearances that gives the lie to the possibility of things *being* what they *seem*. This anxiety may be the response to a theoretical project that radically questions the entire epistemology of interpretation, of the process of understanding and of generating meaning within a text (a text that is itself not above suspicion). It is not that interpretation is rendered impossible (the modernist moment) but, rather, that post-structuralist theory (i.e., the theory developed herein) has bracketed, perhaps temporarily, perhaps not, the suppositions that impel interpretation, putting in its place questions about the function of "interpretation" as a discursive event. Simply put, the question "What does a text mean?" is replaced with questions such as "How does it function?" "Whom does it serve?" "What are its particular investments?" These are questions that do not engender, at least when performed rigorously, simplistic or clear-cut answers, in part because they require that the position from which these questions are asked be interrogated in similar manner.

In a sense, then, the idea of the "margins of theater" invokes that point identified by Lyotard, Kristeva, Derrida, and others at which theater, if only for an imperceptible moment, "produces the highest intensity (by excess or by lack of energy) of what is there, without intention" (Lyotard 1976, 110), at which the theater, rather than "meaning," affirms with an almost Artaudian cruelty the rapturous inculcations of play. As a result, the boundary between hiding and showing is so confounded and combined that any sort of ontological project in the theater becomes nonsensical. In rejecting the ordinate grounds on which meaning is constructed in the "either/or" of the semiotic moment, theater "after post-structuralism," constructs a serial relationship with questions concerning identity that can lead to an "and then . . . and then . . . and then . . . " rhizomatic string (Deleuze and Guattari) that is fundamentally inclusive and excessive in the ways that "signs" are arranged onstage. Simply saying that there is a slippage in the theatrical enterprise that makes anything like a rigid designation between signified and signifier problematic is, to say the least, only telling half the story, is suspending the question of what meanings are possible, and how, indeed, they will function. For within that slippage, there is produced a certain excess of signage that constantly overflows the arid plains of semiotics, constantly adds more to each meaning than can be contained, constantly, as Henry Gates might say, "Signifies" upon the institutionality of theater.

That certain texts can be assigned a place in this uncertain theater would indicate that a theater of the margin retains a relationship to the representational and theatrical structures that it simultaneously problematizes. If, as Andreas Huyssen has argued in *After the Great Divide*, post-structuralist thought articulates the end of modernism by preying on its codes and artifacts inasmuch as it heralds a break with that tradition, then this notion of a theater maintains a similar relationship to the institutional theater. Certainly, like post-structuralism (especially in the configuration I use here), these texts indeed impel something that moves beyond humanist, or universal, experiences, open questions of identity and desire that are inarticulate in the institutional theater (i.e., create terrains hitherto unimaginable). Yet they also relate to textuality, to representation, to closure, in a way that marks and defines the major theater heritage. When Artaud and Nietzsche (as early as *The Birth of Tragedy*) make this argument an explicit dimension of their attacks on what is considered the dominant philosophical tradition in the West, they are onto something similar to Derrida's formulation of theater as repetition of that which does not repeat itself, theatre as the original repetition of difference within the conflict of forces in which "evil is the permanent law and what is good is an effort and already a cruelty added to the other cruelty" [Artaud]—such is the fatal limit of a cruelty which begins with its own representation. (Derrida 1978, 250)

Rather than attempting to solve this opposition, to imagine that some greater moment can, as if by magic (or dialectic), appear to synthesize or reconcile these two disparate ends or to overcome the affirmation inherent in *répétition* with a staid sameness or irony, this theater remains in a state of fractured identity, of multiple possibilities inside and outside, so to speak, a unitary structure.

Nor, of course, is this theater simply limited to the texts I discuss herein, or even to the writers, the "authors," if such a thing is still imaginable or desirable. As I have said, my intention was never to construct a new canon, but merely to suggest some reading strategies that would access a different sensibility from those that have appeared in theater studies so far. Once you accept the rather commonplace notion that an author doesn't really imbue his or her work with an "aura"—a suspect notion for any work of art in or after the age of mechanical reproduction (Benjamin)—but, rather, that a text operates as a complex nexus of institutional, social, and political discourses, that it plays at a multitude of levels, some competing, some contradictory, some institutional, and some affirmative, then the notion of a text as possession gives way to the theatricality of theater, to a sense that the "field of drama" is a playing field and not one to be rigorously (or sloppily) delimited, marked, cultivated, or otherwise colonized in the name of any country, author, or theory.

Perhaps play should be more important than meaning in the theater, perhaps it is more appropriate to "stop making sense" at every level, to reinvest theater with something besides the dull repetition of "old favorites." What would a theater of play, a playful theatrics, entail, if it wanted to do something besides play the same old story, the endless repetition of a "mommy/daddy/me" aesthetic so encoded that it can only preserve and embalm (if not, à la Cixous, actually murder)? Is it possible, at this late moment, to forgo an ontotheological heritage that was, after all, created by people who basically had no use for theater and despised it in any case? Who created a philosophical tradition that sees performance and equivocation as an evil Other to be banished? And who have no use for questions of languages or peoples that do not fit into the numbing simplicity of a world defined by and as Man? Or is the sense-making apparatus endemic to the theater to allow it, as Kathy Acker wants, to "fight this society of death"? If the future of theater is in fact in philosophy, as Brecht argued, then certainly both theater and philosophy must undergo a sea change at some point to manage this futuristic illusion, must reconcile their differences, and see that they are in fact closely related, if not integrally connected, in a syncretic partnership that has nothing to lose but its chains and, indeed, while perhaps still unimaginably so, has worlds to gain.

Notes

Chapter 1

1. Which is not to say that "deconstruction" and "post-structuralist thought" are one and the same or that one is a subset of the other or that they even have any tangible relationship. For that matter, the entire question of defining this movement, complete with authors, texts, and primary subject matters, is an obfuscatory strategy, for the people most often associated with post-structuralist thought are, in actuality, linked only by geographical and historical coincidence. In this light, the connection between deconstruction and post-structuralist thought remains uncertain. Perhaps it is easiest to say that deconstruction concerns itself with unraveling what appears to be the entire system of binary oppositions that create "a text." That is, deconstruction attempts to follow the thread of those binaries in order to ascertain not the true meaning but, rather, the implied assumptions upon which a text rests. Post-structuralist thought concurs with this approach but is concerned not only with writing as linguistic phenomenon but with writing in other historical, structural, political, and sociological forms as well. Clearly, there is a lot more that can be said here, and these definitions are only thumbnail ones at best. I hope that, as this work progresses, the differences and applications of these theories will become more tangible.

2. The term *différance* is crucial to deconstruction. Derrida created the neologism to account for the situation in linguistics that, for Saussure (and subsequent structural linguists), was covered by the terms *signified* and *signifier*. In structural linguistics, this split defines the difference between words and things. Signifiers stand in for signifieds in a complex structure that defines language. According to Derrida, however, the split is not so simple, for words both "defer," or substitute, for the presence of the object or speaker to which they refer, and "differ" from it (and other words simultaneously). Thus, there can never be a one-to-one correlation between signifiers and signifieds because, as a result of this originary "*différance*," there is always slippage—or play, or, even, theatricality—at work in place of any secured meaning.

181

3. Daryl Chin (1989) makes this argument in some detail in reference to the recent productions of Lee Breuer, Peter Brook, and Robert Wilson. His point is that appropriating images, texts, and icons from other cultures willy-nilly, without providing any perspective on their actual cultural function, creates a type of colonizing tourism that makes clear its complicitness with the dominant state apparatus.

4. It is important to note that the "post-structured" stage is indebted to other stages, especially those literary, cultural, and theoretical ones that developed in the 1970s and 1980s under a very general rubric of post-structural thought. The "post-structured stage" has as its fulcrum the hyphen between *post* and *structured,* a diacritical mark that signals both an uneasiness with terminology—the stage is always a contested site—and a desire to keep open the question of who or what will appear on this stage. Like Dada, post-structuralism loses much of its radical potential when it becomes a unified "ism": the hyphen, then, signals a certain disrespect for the more common term *poststructuralism,* which has become the denominator for a certain critical school that came to prominence in the 1970s and 1980s. Post-structuralism itself, as a naming device, is a ruse that perpetuates a certain mastery of meaning and hides the fact that no unifying core of meanings, or hierarchy of signs, effects post-structuralism. The theory that I am expropriating to the theater for this study is a hybrid thought that arises from an overtly French context. While I use a variety of approaches in the pages that follow, I do not follow a theoretical "party line" ("French" or otherwise). I hope to treat theory as a Deleuzeian "toolbox" from which certain approaches to texts can be taken, a toolbox that will put in motion the various lines of thought, including those about theory and theater, that appear here, rather than simply present them as another ruse to seduce the reader into continuing on awhile.

5. The word *play* in the context of Derrida's writing is something of an alien term, for it is not one that he uses, except in *Spurs: Nietzsche's Styles,* after 1967. Furthermore, Derrida uses *jeu* almost exclusively, as Marian Hobson puts it, as "the necessary wobble in a tautly set-up structure" (103) and only rarely, if at all, as "game" or "play." Yet this word is of such primary importance in the theater that it inevitably must be given a wider scope. I want to use it not in the sense of "the free play of the signifier," as several critics have suggested, but, instead, in its Derridian sense of *jeu,* and in a performative sense: "play" not only as a slackness in the machinery but also as a performance designed to beguile whatever audience may be watching.

6. Kirby (1969) explores in some detail the importance and processes of "Happenings." For a more complete understanding of this term than I can provide here, see also Richard Schechner's many articles and books on performance in the 1960s, including *Essays on Performance Theory: 1970–1976.*

7. Kirby's comments here are not as straightforward as they might seem. The issue of critical judgment of a performance piece was the focus of a major debate in theater and performance studies throughout the 1960s, 1970s, and early 1980s, a debate that was played out largely in *TDR, The Drama Review*. On one hand, Kirby, who was editor of *TDR*, felt that all the critic can do is to record, in as objective a fashion as possible, what actually happened onstage, in performance or as ritual, depending on the situation. On the other hand, Richard Schechner, also a longtime editor of *TDR*, felt that it was impossible simply to record without in some way participating in the event. This debate has greatly influenced performance studies in this country, both by determining what "texts" are deemed appropriate for study and, more important, how such texts are studied. This debate was also contemporaneous to a similar one in anthropology. The specifics of this debate can be found in numerous *TDR* editorials from the late 1970s and 1980s.

8. While here I am focusing on only one period of Stein's plays, it is important to keep in mind that her plays ranged from those with a large degree of external referentiality, such as *Yes Is for a Very Young Man*, to those with almost none, such as *Listen to Me*. It is too simple to construct "Gertrude Stein" as a sign for "Language Plays" and leave it at that, for her texts, like any text, are heavily crossed with historical and political investments that are not simply or unproblematically disposed of under the guise of any particular movement. This particular play is useful for my discussion, but, as with any example, numerous other readings of it are possible and, indeed, equally important.

9. Esslin 1987 is a recent example of semiotic theory in a grand sense, for the book attempts a lexiconigraphic overview of the entire field of drama.

10. Mark Poster (1989) analyzes the similarities and differences between the Frankfurt school of cultural theory and French post-structuralist theory in terms of the two critical approaches' understanding of the possibilities for "revolution."

11. Timothy Murray (1989, 207) argues that the differend appears in Rochelle Owens's epistolary play *Chucky's Hunch* as a marker for judging the paternity of traditional drama:

> It is the symbolic value of measure, the Law-of-the-Father, that is here under review. Marked by a tone different from the "awful" judgement of the "old American father," this marginal letter [the only one in the play not written by Chucky], so out of place among Chucky's angry communications, equates the experience of writing with primal reflections on the female scene of creation. This is the enigmatic scene that stands aside—indifference—from the dangerous inheritances of fathers and their maddening dramas. This is the scene "of woman's stye" that Owens' anxious

readers might want to remember amid the maddening spectacle of Chucky's phallic play of letters.

For Murray, the effect of this one letter written by Chucky's mother to his estranged wife, Elly, is to question the ability of the patriarchial discourse set up in the play through Chucky's own ranting letters to account for Elly's experience. Instead, the differend that emerges gives equal voice to the discursive participants (Elly and Chucky) and suggests that a new language structure is necessary in order to legitimate both sides.

12. Jill Dolan (1991) reviews the popular press's reaction to Norman's plays and its attempt to judge her as either a "good" or "bad" playwright according to an imagined Aristotelian position. Dolan makes clear the canonical processes at work as well as the basic absurdity of such a project.

13. For example, see Lyotard's discussion of the disappearance of masternarratives and universals in *The Postmodern Condition* (1984).

14. An additional problem is that Althusser seems too interested in erecting "science" as an alternative to the effects of ideology, without realizing that science has its own ideological interests. For a critique of the "scientific objectivity" that Althusser finally ends up supporting, see Haraway 1989 and 1991. Indeed, her books are more than simply critiques, they rework the relationship between science and technology in terms of gender, race, and postcolonial issues. Both books also contain extensive bibliographies to this new field.

15. Kathleen Woodward (1991, 16) argues, through a close reading of Freud, that aging and old age have remained largely untheorized by otherwise political discourses, a forgetfulness that threatens to render the other categories of political difference willfully hegemonic in regards to old age: "In old age, and in our culture where aging is perceived negatively, old age becomes the dominant category to which we are consigned. If difference produces anxiety, what is the future of difference? For all of us, if we live long enough, that difference is constructed as old age." Certainly, de Lauretis's and Althusser's distinctions are important and necessary steps in understanding the effects of ideology. What I am suggesting by adding Woodward's critique of ageism is that ideology, like power, is diffuse within any cultural location, and, as such, distinguishing the effects of ideology on gender or age only should only be a strategic distinction rather than a categorical prioritization.

16. The recent anthology *Interpreting the Theatrical Past* contains a variety of essays on theater history that address the issues Postlewait and Roach raise. Particularly useful is the extensive bibliography of theater and cultural histography that concludes the book.

17. For examples of a deconstructionist approach to history, see the essays in and Douglas Atkins's introduction to Atkins and Bergeron 1988. In addition, the recent anthology *Critical Theory and Performance* (edited by Janelle G. Reinelt and Joseph R. Roach [1992]) contains several essays that explore this field. It is revealing that in the introduction to the section on "Semiotics and Deconstruction," Janelle Reinelt is able to list three books on semiotics by major theater critics and four journals in which extensive semiotic theater research has been published, but she can name only one journal, *Theatre Journal*, in the area of deconstruction.

Chapter 2

1. Mellencamp 1990 and Sitney 1970 are only two of the many studies of the avant-garde film community of the 1950s and 1960s.

2. See Sitney's description in *Visionary Film*.

3. This film community, with its emphasis on structure and perception, in which Foreman began his theater experiments, is more apropos to the concerns he focuses on than is the theater avant-garde of the period. Both Richard Schechner and Herbert Blau discuss the experimental theater of this period in some detail in various of their books.

4. This is not the place to compare Stein's literary phenomenology with Sartre's, for example, or her notion of "being" with Heidegger's, for example, who argues that it is precisely because of language that presence, and "being" are always impossibilities. See especially Sartre 1956 and Heidegger 1962.

5. Carolyn Talarr pointed out to me that, like T. S. Eliot's footnotes to *The Wasteland*, this pseudo-intellectual catalog of "high philosophy" panders to the masses' desire for knowledge but, in doing so, misrepresents that knowledge.

6. In the printed text, the three main characters, including Estelle Merriweather, are referred to by the first names of the actors who played them in the play's premiere at New York University in 1987.

7. The situation in Frankfurt is not historically isolated. In the Bronx, New York City, during the 1970s, a similar process was occurring as the city consecutively closed down fire stations in crowded areas in order to remove slum housing through fires. For a report on the actual process by which large areas of the South Bronx were decimated, see Wallace 1988. Furthermore, the riots in New York's East Village in 1988 and 1989 were caused by more or less the same problems as those in Frankfurt.

8. In his study of fascism in Germany and Italy, *Fascism and Dictatorship* (1974), Nicos Poulantzas discusses the conditions that led to national socialism in the first instance and draws parallels between fascism and the capital-

ist state. While he resorts to class struggle as the antidote to fascism, his analysis of the fascism in capitalism (and vice versa) parallels Fassbinder's.

9. Kathy Acker's *The Birth of the Poet* explores this point in greater detail. See the next chapter for a further explication.

10. See Deleuze 1990.

11. Kubiak (1987, 78–88) argues that this terrorism is a threat that underlies the very foundations of theater and theatricality.

12. See Kiderlen 1985.

13. A group of about thirty Jews occupied the stage just before the curtain went up, stopping the performance and initiating a verbal battle with the audience and theater personnel. See Kiderlen 1985 for a collection of essays and discussions on the circumstances surrounding the controversy of the 1985 attempt to stage *Garbage, The City and Death*.

14. Letter to Suhrkamp quoted in Zwerenz 1982.

15. Cited in Dadrian 1989, 225. In this article, Dadrian explores the historical situations that led to the Armenian genocide. The precedents that it set for international law were crucial to the prosecution of the individuals responsible for the Holocaust.

16. Both the *Frankfurter Allgemeine Zeitung* and the weekly magazine *Quick* ran articles criticizing Jewish protests. For a summary of this controversy, see Funke 1986, 57–72.

17. At the time, Reagan defended his decision by declaring, "Oh God, I know about [the Holocaust], but do I have to see it?" (quoted in Skelton 1985, 17).

18. According to Lyotard:

The question raised by Auschwitz is that of the texture of the text which "links onto" Auschwitz. If this text is not the speculative one, what might it be? How can it authorize itself, if it is not thanks to the *Umkehrung* [reversal]? It is thanks to the move which passes the thing, the *res* (*die Sache*), from the position of referent in the universe of an unmediated phrase to that of addressor and addressee in the universe of a phrase "linking onto" the preceding one that the second phrase is in effect authorized. It is authorized on account of the fact that what is formulated about the referent of the first phrase is formulated by it (the referent), as addressor, and addressed to it, as addressee. Apart from this movement, how can Auschwitz, something which is thought from the outside, a referent place only "near itself" (*an sich*) (*auprès-de-soi*) "for us" (*für uns*), be interiorized, suppressed . . . as an unmediated position or presupposition, and show itself to itself, know itself in the identity (be it ephemeral) of a for-itself? In the absence of this permutation, there is according to Hegel only chatter, emptiness, subjectivity, arbitrariness, at best regression towards "raciocinative" thought, towards the discourse of the understanding, towards the "modesty" of finitude. (1988, 365)

Although Lyotard makes clear the philosophical resonances of "Auschwitz," it is unclear why "Cambodia" or "Wounded Knee" could not be equally effective "rigid designators" for this model of thought. Consequently, while the model itself is useful as a foundation for the mode of thought signaled by "the differend," the incipient Eurocentricism of the term is unfortunate.

19. Obviously, anti-Semitism exists in many forms and accrues from various sources in various historical periods. It is clearly not enough to say that anti-Semitism exists outside of any historial periodization and that therefore the Holocaust remains a unique rupture. Certainly "Auschwitz" signals an event that is radically incommensurate with "universal history," yet to privilege it as an event rather than a model makes it impossible to accredit other events, such as the Armenian genocide, the Middle Passage, and the Native American genocide, as equally devastating to those who experienced them.

20. For Fassbinder to attempt to speak for the Jewish experience of the Holocaust, that is, to incorporate it into a larger liberal critique of oppression, would serve only to silence Jewish people; to remain silent about the link between fascism and capitalism would only serve to perpetuate the conditions *Garbage, The City and Death* exposes. Unfortunately for Fassbinder, the line between his critique and anti-Semitism is a thin one. On the one hand, it is important not to appropriate the Jewish experience; on the other, it is necessary to acknowledge the Jewish position. In rejecting humanism, Fassbinder also rejects the standard (German) explanations of the Holocaust as an inexplicable lapse; he focuses instead on how it obtains as a consequence of the capitalist state.

Chapter 3

1. Barker (1984) maps the emergence of the private body that is split between sexual desires and productive marketable labor.

2. In fact, could it not be said that the idea of a "fourth wall" onstage, and its contemporary translation into the Stanislavskian "method" of acting, whether the United States or Russian version, creates similar "small theaters" for the actor to enter, to exist in, apparently alone except for the unseen presence of an omniscient audience? And, if so, what more might be said about this particular acting style when political consequences, similar to the ones Foucault pursues in terms of prisons, are examined?

3. Diamond (1990, 59–92) makes a similar argument about the hysteric (and, by extension, women) in realist drama. Diamond's argument is, in part, that the hysteric represents a prime threat to realism's well-ordered

dramatic world and, as such, must either be contained or banished in order for the "well-made play" to continue.

4. A reservation has to be interjected here. It might seem that sexuality became opposed to sex, that, where there was once pleasure, there is now discourse; and that, beyond those discourses, lies the heart of the matter, which consequently requires that sex be rediscovered, as it were, at the expense of sexuality. However, the proliferation of discourses around sex, the multiplication of variations of sexualities, has in fact further integrated sex and sexuality. Rather than producing pleasure, sex produces discourses about sex, discourses that are vehicles for the effects of power. Foucault argues that these discourses have not produced a repression of sex but, rather, have replaced pleasure with power, with the instigation of an objective criterion for sex that designates it as another terrain wherein power resides. Ultimately, sexuality and sex intermingle; power conflates the boundaries between them until they are inseparable, yet distinct, entities. Furthermore, the apparent binarization of *ars erotica* and *Scientia Sexualis* is misleading, for in fact they exist as two mutually distinct categories that do not share a competitive moment.

5. It is this discursivity that Barker (1984) suggests is constructed as negative and thus excluded from discourse. Foucault (1980a) makes a similar argument.

6. In the first U.S. production at the Brooklyn Academy of Music, the lines not assigned to particular characters (like these) were read aloud over the public address system (cited in Fuchs 1989, 20–45).

7. See chapter 2.

8. Due to the physical limitations of the software on which this chapter was composed, I am omitting the Arabic script that appears in the printed version of the play above and to the right (Arabic reads right to left) of the Roman transliterations. I regret this omission and take full responsibility for its implied "Orientalism."

9. The treatment of witches, on the one hand, and "Arabs," on the other, is well documented. Said 1978 is a major text in this regard. Derrida (1986) discusses the implications of the word *apartheid* in terms of its significance to the production of racism.

Chapter 4

1. *Master-narrative* is Lyotard's term for the "great narratives"—such as emancipation, speculation, and legitimation of knowledge—that have structured thought in the modern period. These narratives have been held up as elements to which all thought must aspire and by which all thought is judged. In enunciating a "post-modern" condition, Lyotard argues that these

narratives are no longer legitimate as arbitrators of thought because, quite simply, all thought and/or experience cannot be encompassed within the (Eurocentric) metaphysical framework that created these narratives. See Lyotard 1984.

2. While it may seem strange to suddenly assert success in the "mainstream" as the primary criterion for acceptance, to a certain extent such recognition does determine what plays are published and therefore are available to a national audience. This is not to say, however, that such recognition imputes any artistic merit or hierarchy between widely produced and more obscure plays. Certainly, by the standards of most regional repertory theaters or bookstores, the two plays I consider in this chapter are obscure. Yet the critics who write about these plays and playwrights make their work more readily available and therefore contribute to those works' and authors' entry into the mainstream.

3. Tisa Chang's *The Return of the Phoenix* (1974), Benny Ye and Nobuko Miyamoto's *Chop Suey* (1980), Philip Kan Gotanda's *Yankee Dawg You Die* (1988), and Chin's two plays *The Chickencoop Chinaman* (1984) and *Year of the Dragon* (1984) have also reached national recognition in "alternative" circles.

4. *AIIIEEEE!* was the first Asian American literary journal in the United States.

5. See Yarbro-Bejarano 1986a, 44–58.

6. "*Chingar* then is to do violence to another, i.e. rape. The verb is masculine, active, cruel: it stings, wounds, gashes, stains. . . . The person who suffers this action is passive, inert, and open, in contrast to the active, aggressive, and closed person who inflicts it. The *chingón* is the macho, the male; he rips open the chingada, the female, who is pure passivity, defenseless against the exterior world" (Octavio Paz, quoted in Yarbro-Bejarano 1986b, 393).

7. See Yarbro-Bejarano 1986b, 393: "Chicanas who question traditional gender roles and attempt to organize their desire independently run the risk of being labeled *malinchistas.*"

8. The usage of the name *Malinche* varies in this passage because Yvonne Yarbro-Bejarano uses *La Malinche* more as an image or figure and Nancy Saporta Sternbach uses *Malinche* more as a historical person. I want to maintain this difference only on a practical level, however, for their theoretical use of the name in fact varies little.

9. Indeed, the role of the *bato* in establishing Chicano culture as a viable, vibrant force both inside and outside the barrio should not be underestimated. Certainly, it is only one of many forces at work within that community, but, from the Zoot Suit riots in Los Angeles in the 1940s to the lowriders of the 1980s and 1990s, *batos* have represented a certain "in your face" attitude that has made ignoring Chicano culture largely impossible. This isn't to say,

of course, that *batos* represent in any way the entirety, or even the most politically important, dimensions of Chicano culture.

10. See Baudrillard 1983a, 18: "Seduction doesn't recuperate the autonomy of the body . . . truth . . . the sovereignty of this seduction is transsexual, not bisexual, destroying all sexual organization."

11. See Rubin 1975, 157–210.

12. An example of such a movement is the Black American tradition of "Signifyin(g)," in which the tropes of the dominant culture are themselves troped, a process that reveals a profound fluidity within the original sign that threatens that sign's ability to structure discourse.

13. Daryl Chin's analysis of Lee Breuer's *The Warrior Ant* ("Interculturalism, Postmodernism, Pluralism" [1989]) suggests that, in Breuer's wholesale appropriation of various performance elements, a similar loss of the cultural specificity of each element occurs: "This disjunction [of elements] ultimately devalued all elements, as no element was allowed to exist within an appropriate context; appropriate, that is, in terms of the cultural context from which that element derived" (168). Such borrowings simply promulgate the blindness to the Other by collapsing any cultural difference into a hegemonic indifference.

14. In *Spurs: Nietzsche's Styles,* while reading one of Nietzsche's manuscripts, Derrida comes across a note in the margin: "I have forgotten my umbrella." What Derrida infers from this note is that there is no way to be sure that Nietzsche didn't "mean" for the note to be there, or, more important, that whether Nietzsche meant for it to be there or not, it is, and thus cannot be ignored simply because it is on the margin. From this, Derrida suggests that a text can be opened infinitely, a point I work through in chapter 1. My point here in obliquely invoking Derrida's reading of Nietzsche is to suggest both that what was hitherto on the margin needs to be read not as "marginalia" but as "text" and, furthermore, that when theory tries to act as an umbrella by covering everything, it is always, pace Derrida, in for a surprise. (See chap. 1.)

15. "So-called humanism" is Henry Louis Gates's reply to the inability of humanism to account for non-Anglo-European voices. See Gates 1989, 324–46.

Bibliography

Acker, Kathy. "Realism for the Cause of Future Revolution." In *Art after Modernism: Rethinking Representation,* edited by Brian Wallis. New York: New Museum of Contemporary Art, 1984.

———. *The Birth of the Poet.* In *Wordplays 5,* edited by Bonnie Marranca and Gautam Dasgupta. New York: PAJ Publications, 1986.

Alarcón, Norma. "Making Familia from Scratch: Split Subjectivities in the Work of Helena Maria Viramontes and Cherríe Moraga." In *Chicana Creativity and Criticism: Charting New Frontiers in American Literature,* edited by Maria Herrera-Sobek and Helena Maria Viramontes. Houston: Arte Publico, 1988.

Althusser, Louis. *For Marx.* Translated by Ben Brewster. New York: Allen Lane, 1969.

———. *Lenin and Philosophy.* Translated by Ben Brewster. New York: Monthly Review Press, 1971.

Anderson, Perry. *In the Tracks of Historical Materialism.* London: Verso, 1983.

———. "Modernity and Revolution." In *Marxism and the Interpretation of Culture,* edited by Lawrence Grossberg and Cary Nelson. Urbana: University of Illinois Press, 1988.

Arac, Jonathan. *Critical Genealogies: Historical Situations for Postmodern Literary Studies.* New York: Columbia University Press, 1987a.

———, ed. *Postmodernism and Politics.* Minneapolis: University of Minnesota Press, 1987b.

Artaud, Antonin. *The Theatre and Its Double.* Translated by Mary Caroline Richards. New York: Grove Press, 1958.

———. *Oeuvres complètes.* Paris: Gallimard, 1970.

Atkins, Douglas G., and David M. Bergeron, eds. *Shakespeare and Deconstruction.* New York: Peter Lang, 1988.

Attridge, Derek, Geoff Bennington, and Robert Young, eds. *Post-Structuralism and the Question of History.* New York: Cambridge University Press, 1987.

Barker, Francis. *The Tremulous Private Body: Essays on Subjection.* New York: Methuen, 1984.

Barthes, Roland. *Critical Essays.* Translated by Richard Howard. Evanston, Ill.: Northwestern University Press, 1972.

———. *Empire of Signs.* Translated by Richard Howard. London: Macmillan, 1974a.

————. *Image-Music-Text*. Translated by Stephen Heath. New York: Hill and Wang, 1974b.

————. *S/Z*. Translated by Richard Miller. New York: Hill and Wang, 1974c.

————. *Roland Barthes by Roland Barthes*. Translated by Richard Howard. London: Macmillan, 1977.

Baudrillard, Jean. "Our Theatre of Cruelty." *Semiotext(e)* 4 (1982): 105–9.

————. "The Ecstasy of Communication." In *The Anti-Aesthetic: Essays on Postmodern Culture*, edited by Hal Foster. Port Townsend, Wash.: Bay Press, 1983a.

————. *In the Shadow of the Silent Majorities*. Translated by Paul Foss, Paul Patton, and Phillip Beitchman. New York: Semiotext(e), 1983b.

————. *Simulations*. Translated by Paul Foss, Paul Patton, and Phillip Beitchman. New York: Semiotext(e), 1983c.

————. *Forget Foucault*. Translated by Nicole Dufresne. New York: Semiotext(e), 1987.

Benmussa, Simone. "Introduction." In *Benmussa Directs*, translated by Anita Barrows. Dallas: Riverrun Press, 1979.

Bennington, Geoffrey. *Lyotard: Writing the Event*. New York: Columbia University Press, 1988.

Birringer, Johannes. " 'Medea': Landscapes beyond History." *New German Critique*, no. 50 (Spring/Summer 1990): 85–112.

Blanchot, Maurice. *Le Pas au-dela*. Paris: Gallimard, 1973.

Blau, Herbert. *Blooded Thought: Occasions of Theatre*. New York: PAJ Publications, 1982a.

————. *Take Up the Bodies: Theatre at the Vanishing Point*. Urbana: University of Illinois Press, 1982b.

————. "Ideology and Performance." *Theatre Journal* 35, no. 4 (December 1983): 441–60.

————. *The Audience*. Baltimore: Johns Hopkins University Press, 1990.

Brecht, Bertolt. *Brecht on Theatre*. Edited and translated by John Willett. New York: Hill and Wang, 1964.

Breton, André. *Manifestos of Surrealism*. Translated by Helen R. Lane and Richard Seaver. Ann Arbor: University of Michigan Press, 1969.

Brewer, Maria Minich. "Performing Theory." *Theatre Journal* 37, no. 1 (March 1985): 13–30.

Butler, Judith. *Gender Trouble: Feminism and the Subversion of Identity*. New York: Routledge, 1990.

Carlson, Marvin. *The Semiotics of Theatre: Signs of Life*. Bloomington: Indiana University Press, 1990.

Chin, Daryl. "Interculturalism, Postmodernism, Pluralism." *Performing Arts Journal* 11, no. 3/12, no. 1 (1989): 163–75.

Chin, Frank. *The Chickencoop Chinaman*. Seattle: University of Washington Press, 1984.

Chin, Frank, Jeffery Paul Chan, and Shawn Wong, eds. *Anthology of Asian-American Writers*. Garden City, N.Y.: Doubleday Press, 1975.

Christian, Barbara. "The Race for Theory." *Cultural Critique* 6 (March 1987): 51–65.

Churchill, Caryl. *Softcops*. New York: Methuen, 1984.

Churchill, Caryl, and David Lan. *A Mouthful of Birds*. London: Methuen, 1986.

Cixous, Hélène. "Portrait of Dora." In *Benmussa Directs*, translated by Anita Barrows. Dallas: Riverrun Press, 1979.

———. "Ala à la mer." *Modern Drama* 27, no. 4 (December 1984): 546–48.

Culler, Jonathan. *Structuralist Poetics: Structuralist Linguistics and the Study of Literature*. New York: Routledge, 1975.

Dadrian, Vahakn N. "Genocide as a Problem of National and International Law: The World War I Armenian Case and Its Contemporary Legal Ramifications." *Yale Journal of International Law* 14, no. 2 (Summer 1989): 221–334.

de Lauretis, Teresa. *Alice Doesn't: Feminism, Semiotics, Cinema*. Bloomington: University of Indiana Press, 1984.

———. *Technologies of Gender*. Bloomington: University of Indiana Press, 1987.

———. "Sexual Indifference and Lesbian Representation." *Theatre Journal* 40, no. 2 (May 1988): 155–77.

Debord, Guy. *Society of the Spectacle*. Detroit: Red and Black, n.d.

Deleuze, Gilles. *Nietzsche*. Translated by Hugh Tomlison. New York: Columbia University Press, 1982.

———. *Foucault*. Translated by Sean Hand. Minneapolis: University of Minnesota Press, 1988.

———. *The Logic of Sense*. Translated by Mark Lester. New York: Columbia University Press, 1990.

Deleuze, Gilles, and Félix Guattari. *Anti-Oedipus: Capitalism and Schizophrenia*. Translated by Robert Hurley, Mark Seem, and Helen R. Lane. Minneapolis: University of Minnesota Press, 1983.

———. *A Thousand Plateaus: Capitalism and Schizophrenia*. Translated with a foreword by Brian Massumi. Minneapolis: University of Minnesota Press, 1987.

Derrida, Jacques. *Writing and Difference*. Translated by Alan Bass. Chicago: University of Chicago Press, 1978.

———. *Spurs: Nietzsche's Styles/Eprons: les style de Nietzsche*. Translated by Barbara Harlow. Chicago: University of Chicago Press, 1980.

———. *Positions*. Translated by Alan Bass. Chicago: University of Chicago Press, 1981.

———. *Dissemination*. Translated by Barbara Johnson. Chicago: University of Chicago Press, 1982a.

———. *Margins of Philosophy*. Translated by Alan Bass. Chicago: University of Chicago Press, 1982b.

———. "The Last Word in Racism." In *Race, Writing, and Difference*, edited by Henry Louis Gates. Chicago: University of Chicago Press, 1986.

Diamond, Elin. "(In)Visible Bodies in Churchill's Theatre." In *Making a Spectacle: Feminist Essays on Contemporary Women's Theatre*, edited by Lynda Hart. Ann Arbor: University of Michigan Press, 1989a.

———. "Mimesis, Mimicry, and the 'True-Real.'" *Modern Drama* 32, no. 1 (1989b): 58–72.

———. "Realism and Hysteria: Toward a Feminist Mimesis." *Discourse* 13, no. 1 (September 1990): 59–92.

Diamond, Irene, and Lee Quinby, eds. *Feminism and Foucault: Reflections on Resistance*. Boston: Northeastern University Press, 1988.

Dolan, Jill. *The Feminist Spectator as Critic*. 1988. Reprint. Ann Arbor: University of Michigan Press, 1991.

Eagleton, Terry. *Literary Theory: An Introduction*. Minneapolis: University of Minnesota Press, 1983.

Elam, Kier. *The Semiotics of Theatre and Drama*. New York: Methuen, 1980.

Esslin, Martin. *The Field of Drama: How the Signs of Drama Create Meaning on Stage and Screen*. New York: Methuen, 1987.

Fassbinder, Rainer Werner. "Interview." *Theater Heute* 5 (August 1976): 14.

———. *Blood on the Cat's Neck. Five Plays by Rainer Werner Fassbinder*. Edited and translated by Dennis Calandra. New York: PAJ Publications, 1985a.

———. *Garbage, The City and Death. Five Plays by Rainer Werner Fassbinder*. Edited and translated by Dennis Calandra. New York: PAJ Publications, 1985b.

Féral, Josette. "Writing and Displacement: Women in Theatre." *Modern Drama* 27, no. 4 (December 1984): 549–59.

Foreman, Richard. *The Ontological Hysteric Theatre: Plays and Manifestos*. New York: PAJ Publications, 1976.

———. "Pandering to the Masses: A Misrepresentation." In *Theatre of Images*, edited by Bonnie Marranca. New York: PAJ Publications, 1977.

———. *Reverberation Machines: The Later Plays and Essays*. Barrytown, N.Y.: Station Hill Press, 1985.

———. "Film Is Evil: Radio Is Good." *TDR* T116 (December 1987): 149–76.

Foucault, Michel. *The Order of Things: An Archaeology of the Human Sciences*. Translated by Alan Sheridan. New York: Random House, 1970.

———. *Language, Counter-Memory, Practice*. Edited and translated by Donald F. Bouchard. Ithaca, N.Y.: Cornell University Press, 1977.

———. *Discipline and Punish: The Birth of the Prison*. Translated by Alan Sheridan. New York: Pantheon, 1979.

———. *The History of Sexuality*, vol. 1. Translated by Robert Hurley. New York: Pantheon, 1980a.

———. *Power/Knowledge: Selected Interviews and Other Writings, 1972–1977*. Edited and translated by Colin Gordon. New York: Pantheon, 1980b.

———. *Foucault Live (Interviews, 1966–1984)*. Edited by Sylvere Lotringer; translated by John Johnson. New York: Semiotext(e), 1989.

Froula, Christine. "When Eve Reads Milton: Undoing the Canonical Economy." In *Canons*, edited by Robert von Halberg. Chicago: University of Chicago Press, 1984.

Fuchs, Elinor. "Staging the Obscene Body." *TDR* T121 (Spring 1989): 35–54.

Funke, Hajo. "Bitburg, Jews, and Germans: A Case Study of Anti-Jewish Sentiment in Germany during May, 1985." *New German Critique* 26 (March 1986): 57–72.

Gates, Henry Louis, Jr. "Writing 'Race' and the Difference It Makes." *Critical Inquiry* 12, no. 1 (1985): 1–20.

———. "Authority, (White) Power, and the (Black) Critic; or, It's All Greek to Me." In *The Future of Literary Theory*, edited by Ralph Cohen. New York: Routledge, 1989.

Geertz, Clifford. *Works and Lives: The Anthropologist as Author*. Stanford, Calif.: Stanford University Press, 1988.

González, Yolanda Broyles. "Towards a Re-Vision of Chicano Theatre History: The Women of El Teatro Campesion." In *Making a Spectacle: Feminist Essays on Contemporary Women's Theatre*, edited by Lynda Hart. Ann Arbor: University of Michigan Press, 1989.

Haraway, Donna J. *Primate Visions: Gender, Race, and Nature in the World of Modern Science*. New York: Routledge, 1989.

———. *Simians, Cyborgs, and Women: The Reinvention of Nature*. New York: Routledge, 1991.

Hays, Michael. "Theatre History and Practice: An Alternative View of Drama." *New German Critique*, no. 12 (Fall 1977): 85–98.

Heidegger, Martin. *Being and Time*. Translated by John Macquarrie and Edward Robinson. New York: Harper and Row, 1962.

———. *What Is a Thing?* Translated by W. B. Barton and Vera Deutsch. South Bend, Ind.: Regnery, Gateway, 1967.

Herrera-Sobek, Maria. "The Politics of Rape: Sexual Transgression in Chicana Fiction." In *Chicana Creativity and Criticism: Charting New Frontiers in American Literature*, edited by Maria Herrera-Sobek and Helena Maria Viramontes. Houston: Arte Publico, 1988.

Hobson, Marian. "History Traces." In *Post-Structuralism and the Question of History*, edited by Derek Attridge, Geoffrey Bennington, and Robert Young. New York: Cambridge University Press, 1987.

Huerta, Jorge. *Chicano Theatre: Themes and Forms*. Ypsilanti, Calif.: Bilingual Press, 1982.

Huyssen, Andreas. *After the Great Divide: Modernism, Mass Culture, Postmodernism*. Bloomington: Indiana University Press, 1986.

Irigaray, Luce. *This Sex Which Is Not One*. Translated by Cathrine Porter and Carolyn Burke. Ithaca, N.Y.: Cornell University Press, 1979.

———. *L'Oubli de l'air chez Martin Heidegger*. Paris: Minuit, 1983.

———. *Speculum of the Other Woman*. Translated by Gillian C. Gill. Ithaca, N.Y.: Cornell University Press, 1985.

Jameson, Fredric. *The Political Unconscious: Narrative as a Socially Symbolic Act*. Ithaca, N.Y.: Cornell University Press, 1981.

————. "Postmodernism; or, The Cultural Logic of Late Capitalism." *New Left Review* 146 (July 1984): 53–92.

Kiderlen, Hans, ed. *Deutsch-jüdische Normalität . . . Fassbinder's Sprengsätze.* Frankfurt am Main: Pflasterstrand GmBH, 1985.

Kim, Elaine H. "Defining Asian American Realities through Literature." *Cultural Critique* 6 (1987): 87–111.

————. "'Such Opposite Creatures': Men and Women in Asian American Literature." *Michigan Quarterly Review* 29, no. 1 (Winter 1990): 68–93.

Kirby, Michael. *The Art of Time: Essays on the Avant-Garde.* New York: E. P. Dutton, 1969.

————. *A Formalist Theatre.* Philadelphia: University of Pennsylvania Press, 1987.

Kowsar, Mohammad. "Althusser on Theatre." *Theatre Journal* 35, no. 4 (December 1983): 461–74.

Krieger, Murray. *Words about Words about Words: Theory, Criticism, and the Literary Text.* Baltimore: Johns Hopkins University Press, 1988.

Kristeva, Julia. "Modern Theatre Does Not Take (A) Place." *Sub-Stance* 18–19 (1977): 131–34.

————. *Powers of Horror: An Essay on Abjection.* Translated by Leon S. Roudiez. New York: Columbia University Press, 1982.

Kubiak, Anthony. "Disappearance as History: The Stages of Terror." *Theatre Journal* 39, no. 1 (March 1987): 78–88.

Lacoue-Labarthe, Philippe. *Heidegger, Art, and Politics: The Fiction of the Political.* Translated by Chris Turner. New York: Basil Blackwell, 1990.

Lamont, Rosette C. "The Reverse Side of a Portrait: The Dora of Freud and Cixous." In *Feminine Focus: The New Women Playwrights,* edited by Enoch Brater. New York: Oxford University Press, 1989.

Li, David Leiwei. *The Formation of Frank Chin and Formations of Chinese American Literature.* Pullman: Washington State University Press, 1991.

Lim, Shirley Geok-lin. "Twelve Asian American Writers in Search of Self-Definition." *Melus* 13, nos. 1–2 (March 1986): 57–78.

Ling, Amy. "A Perspective on Chinamerican Literature." *Melus* 8, no. 2 (June 1981): 76–81.

————. "Asian American Literature." In *Redefining American Literary History,* edited by A. LaVonne Brown Ruoff and Jerry W. Ward. New York: Modern Language Association of America, 1990.

Lorde, Audre. "An Open Letter to Mary Daly." In *This Bridge Called My Back: Writings by Radical Women of Color,* edited by Cherríe Moraga and Gloria Anzalduá. New York: Kitchen Table Press, 1981.

Lyotard, Jean-François. "The Tooth, the Palm." *Sub-Stance* 15 (1976): 105–10.

————. *The Post Modern Condition: A Report on Knowledge.* Translated by Brian Massumi. Minneapolis: University of Minnesota Press, 1984.

————. *The Differend: Phrases in Dispute.* Translated by George Van Abeele. Minneapolis: University of Minnesota Press, 1988.

MacDonald, Dorothy. "An Introduction to Frank Chin's 'The Chickencoop Chinaman' and 'The Year of the Dragon.'" In *Essays in Chicano, Native American, and Asian-American Literature for Teachers of American Literature,* edited by Houston Baker. New York: Modern Language Association of America, 1982.

Marranca, Bonnie, ed. *Theatre of Images.* New York: PAJ Publications, 1977.

Mellencamp, Patricia. *Indiscretions: Avant-Garde Film, Video, and Feminism.* Bloomington: University of Indiana Press, 1990.

Melville, Margarita B. "Female and Male in Chicano Theatre." In *Hispanic Theatre in the United States,* edited by Nicolas Kanellos. Houston: Arte Publico, 1984.

Moraga, Cherríe. *Giving Up the Ghost.* Los Angeles: West End Press, 1986.

Moy, James. "David Henry Hwang's *M. Butterfly* and Philip Kan Gotanda's *Yankee Dawg You Die:* Repositioning Chinese-American Marginality on the American Stage." *Theatre Journal* 42, no. 3 (October 1990): 302–20.

Müller, Heiner. "Die Notwendige Zumtung." *Theater Heute* 10 (August 1984a): 10.

———. *Hamletmachine.* In *Hamletmachine and Other Texts for the Stage,* edited by Carl Weber. New York: Performing Arts Publications, 1984b.

Murray, Timothy. "Patriarchal Panopticism, or The Seduction of a Bad Joke: Getting Out in Theory." *Theatre Journal* 35, no. 3 (October 1983): 376–88.

———. "Screening the Camera's Eye: Black and White Confrontations of Technological Representation." *Modern Drama* 28, no. 1 (March 1985): 110–24.

———. *Theatrical Legitimation: Allegories of Genius in Seventeenth-Century England and France.* New York: Oxford University Press, 1987.

———. "The Play of Letters: Possession and Writing in *Chucky's Hunch.*" In *Feminine Focus: The New Women Playwrights,* edited by Enoch Brater. New York: Oxford University Press, 1989.

Nägele, Rainer. *Theater, Theory, Speculation: Walter Benjamin and the Scenes of Modernity.* Baltimore: Johns Hopkins University Press, 1991.

Nietzsche, Friedrich. *Beyond Good and Evil.* Translated by R. J. Hollingdale. New York: Vintage Books, 1967.

Ordóñez, Elizabeth J. "The Concept of Cultural Identity in Chicana Poetry." *Third Woman* 2, no. 1 (1984): 75–82.

Pavis, Patrice. *Languages of the Stage: Essays in the Semiology of Theatre.* New York: PAJ Publications, 1982.

Phelan, Peggy. "Feminist Theory, Post-Structuralism, and Performance." *TDR* T123 (September 1988): 109–26.

Poster, Mark. *Critical Theory and Poststructuralism: In Search of a Context.* Ithaca, N.Y.: Cornell University Press, 1989.

Postlewait, Thomas. "Historiography and the Theatrical Event: A Primer with Twelve Cruxes." *Theatre Journal* 43, no. 21 (May 1991): 157–78.

Poulantzas, Nicos. *Fascism and Dictatorship.* London: NLB, 1974.

Radhakrishnan, R. "Ethnic Identity and Post-Structuralist Difference." *Critical Inquiry* 12, no. 1 (1985): 199–220.

Reinelt, Janelle G., and Joseph R. Roach, eds. *Critical Theory and Performance.* Ann Arbor: University of Michigan Press, 1992.

Roach, Joseph. *The Player's Passion: Studies in the Science of Acting.* Cranbury, N.J.: Associated University Presses, 1985.

Roth, Moira. *The Amazing Decade: Women and Performance Art in America, 1970–1980.* Los Angeles: Astro Artz, 1983.

Rubin, Gayle. "The Traffic in Women: Notes on the 'Political Economy' of Sex." In *Towards an Anthropology of Women,* edited by Chris Reiter. New York: Monthly Review Press, 1975.

Ryan, Michael. *Marxism and Deconstruction: A Critical Articulation.* Baltimore: Johns Hopkins University Press, 1982.

Said, Edward. *Orientalism.* New York: Random House, 1978.

Sartre, Jean-Paul. *Being and Nothingness: An Essay on Phenomenological Ontology.* Translated and introduced by Hazel E. Barnes. New York: Philosophical Library, 1956.

Savona, Jeannette Laillou. "In Search of a Feminist Theatre: Portrait of Dora." In *Feminine Focus: The New Women Playwrights,* edited by Enoch Brater. New York: Oxford University Press, 1989.

Schechner, Richard. *Essays on Performance Theory: 1970–1976.* New York: Drama Specialists, 1977.

Shaviro, Steven. *Passion and Excess: Blanchot, Bataille, and Literary Theory.* Tallahassee: Florida State University Press, 1990.

Shawn, Wallace. *A Thought in Three Parts.* In *Wordplays 2,* edited by Bonnie Marranca and Guatam Dasgupta. New York: PAJ Publications, 1983.

Sitney, P. Adam. *Visionary Film: The American Avant-Garde, 1943–1968.* New York: Oxford University Press, 1970.

Skelton, George. "Image of Blundering Fought: Can Eloquence Calm the Furor? Aids to Wait, See." *Los Angeles Times,* 6 May 1985, 17.

Sloterdijk, Peter. *Thinker on Stage: Nietzsche's Materialism.* Translated by Jamie Owen Daniel. Minneapolis: University of Minnesota Press, 1989.

Smith, Barbara Herrnstein. "Contingencies of Value." In *Canons,* edited by Robert von Halberg. Chicago: University of Chicago Press, 1984.

Spivak, Gayatri Chakavorty. "Can the Subaltern Speak?" In *Marxism and the Interpretation of Culture,* edited by Lawrence Grossberg and Cary Nelson. Urbana: University of Illinois Press, 1988.

Stein, Gertrude. *The Geographical History of America or the Relation of Human Nature to the Human Mind.* New York: Random House, 1973.

———. *Listen to Me. Last Operas and Plays.* Edited by Carl Van Vechten. New York: Vintage Books, 1975.

Sternbach, Nancy Saporta. "'A Deep Racial Memory of Love': The Chicana Feminism of Cherríe Moraga." In *Breaking Boundaries: Latina Writing and Critical Readings,* edited by Asuncion Horno-Delgado, Eliana Ortega, Nina

M. Scott, and Nancy Saporta Sternbach. Amherst: University of Massachusetts Press, 1989.

Trinh, T. Minh-ha. *Woman, Native, Other.* Bloomington: Indiana University Press, 1989.

Ubersfeld, Anne. *Lire le théâtre.* Paris: Editions Sociales, 1977.

Valdes, Guadalupe. "Language Attitudes and Their Reflection in Chicano Theatre: An Exploratory Study." *New Scholar: An Americanist Review* 8, nos. 1–2 (1988): 181–200.

Veltrusky, Jiri. "Man and Object in the Theatre." In *A Prague School Reader on Esthetics, Literary Structure and Style,* edited by Paul L. Garvin. Washington, D.C.: Georgetown University Press, 1964.

Wallace, Rodrick. "A Synergism of Plagues: 'Planned Shrinkage,' Contagious Housing Destruction, and AIDS in the Bronx." *Environmental Research* 47 (1988): 215–18.

Woodward, Kathleen. "Introduction." *Discourse* 13, no. 1 (September 1990): 3–11.

———. *Aging and Its Discontents: Freud and Other Fictions.* Bloomington: Indiana University Press, 1991.

Yarbro-Bejarano, Yvonne. "Chicanas' Experience in Collective Theatre: Ideology and Form." *Women and Performance* 2, no. 2 (1986a): 44–58.

———. "The Female Subject in Chicano Theatre: Sexuality, 'Race,' and Class." *Theatre Journal* 38, no. 4 (December 1986b): 389–407.

Zwerenz, Gerhard. *Der Langsame Tod des Rainer Werner Fassbinder.* Munich: Knaur, 1982.

Index